Meditations on *Metamorphosis*

Steven Berkoff is an actor, director and playwright. His plays include
East, West, Sink the Belgrano!, Decadence, Kvetch, Greek and *Acapulco*.
His work also includes two theatre journals, *I Am Hamlet* and
Coriolanus in Deutschland, a collection of essays, *Overview*, adaptations
of Kafka's *Metamorphosis* and *The Trial*, and his own film, *Decadence*.

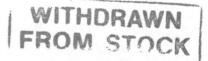

STEVEN BERKOFF

Meditations on *Metamorphosis*

faber and faber

First published in 1995 by
Faber and Faber Limited 3 Queen Square London WC1N 3AU

Photoset by Parker Typesetting Service, Leicester
Printed by Antony Rowe Ltd,
Eastbourne, England.

A CIP record for this book
is available from the British Library

ISBN 0–571–17629–1

For Clara

Contents

List of Illustrations

Acknowledgements

A special thanks to Brenda Watkinson for typing, correcting and going over the manuscript with her usual eagle eye. I should also like to thank all the actors who have performed in the various productions. My gratitude to Susumi Matahira for making all this possible along with the Japanese cast mentioned in the following pages for giving me such a warm welcome in their country. Finally, I should like to dedicate the book to the memory of Brad Davis who played Gregor at the Mark Taper Forum in Los Angeles with such vitality, combined with an unusual tenderness.

Productions of *Metamorphosis*

1969 – *The Round House, London*

GREGOR SAMSA	Steven Berkoff
MR SAMSA	George Little
MRS SAMSA	Jean James
GRETA	Petra Markham
CHIEF CLERK/LODGER	Chris Munke

1976 – *National Theatre, London, and tour*

GREGOR SAMSA	Terry McGinity
MR SAMSA	Steven Berkoff
MRS SAMSA	Maggie Jordan
GRETA	Mary Rutherford
CHIEF CLERK	Barry Philips
LODGER	Matthew Scurfield

1976 – *Nimrod Theatre, Sydney*

GREGOR SAMSA	Ralph Cotterill
MR SAMSA	George Shevtsov
MRS SAMSA	Janice Finn
GRETA	Margaret Cameron
CHIEF CLERK	Paul Bertram
LODGER	Richard Collins

1978 – *Haifa, Israel*

GREGOR SAMSA	Asher Sarfaty
MR SAMSA	Ilan Toren
MRS SAMSA	Devorah Keidar
GRETA	Leora Rivlin
CHIEF CLERK/LODGER	Shmuel Wolff

1982 – *Los Angeles*

GREGOR SAMSA Brad Davis
MR SAMSA Pat McNamara
MRS SAMSA Priscilla Smith
GRETA Annabella Price
CHIEF CLERK/LODGER Ebbe Roe-Smith

1983 – *Düsseldorf*

GREGOR SAMSA Bernd Jeschek
MR SAMSA Karlheinz Vietsch
MRS SAMSA Bigi Fischer
GRETA Christiane Gött
CHIEF CLERK/LODGER Michael Prelle

1986 – *The Mermaid Theatre, London*

GREGOR SAMSA Tim Roth
MR SAMSA Steven Berkoff
MRS SAMSA Linda Marlowe
GRETA Saskia Reeves
CHIEF CLERK/LODGER Gary Olsen

1988 – *Paris*

GREGOR SAMSA Roman Polanski
MR SAMSA Fred Personne
MRS SAMSA Christiane Cohendy
GRETA Fabienne Tricottet
CHIEF CLERK/LODGER Jean-Paul Farre

1989 – *Broadway, New York*

GREGOR SAMSA Mikhail Baryshnikov
MR SAMSA René Auberjonois
MRS SAMSA Laura Esterman
GRETA Madeleine Potter
CHIEF CLERK Mitch Kreindel
LODGER T. J. Meyers

1992 – *Mitsubishi Theatre, Tokyo*

GREGOR SAMSA Amon Miyamoto
MR SAMSA Masumi Okada
MRS SAMSA Mari Natsuki
GRETA Atsuko Takaizumi
CHIEF CLERK Makoto Yuasa
LODGER Yuji Nakamura

Introduction

I knew it would be impossible to continue a career in the theatre as an actor waiting like a lottery ticket holder for my number to come up. Sometimes I had splendid runs of luck and entered characters I would never have thought of choosing of my own free will and was stretched by such experiences. Then there would be endless gulfs of time when frustration mixed with the guilt of being a fit yet unemployed man made a cocktail that was bitter to taste. During such periods I decided to search for a means of choosing my own destiny and become an actor in search of an author. I chose *Metamorphosis* by Franz Kafka as a means of defining who I was as an actor and director. I wanted to exercise the possibility of an actor being stretched beyond the pale of naturalism and to create theatre that was truly theatrical, that penetrated beneath the surface of human activity with its simple human conflicts and ego-bound convention that obsesses most playwrights. What is so haunting about Kafka's vision is that it is the vision of the condemned man who views every fragment of his universe with unconcealed intensity, even if the mood is sometimes cool and austere.

In a hot rehearsal room in the summer of '69, I and a small group of actors began blocking the play, and the form gradually emerged. This journal is a record of the actors who have taken this journey with me in over ten productions, ending up in Tokyo – the scene of the final and definitive one.

The first performance took place at the Roundhouse, London's famous 'engine turning shed', and for that I thank Arnold Wesker who rescued this formidable building, now, alas, lost. I shall never forget those three short weeks when we played in a blistering heatwave to packed houses and which confirmed my belief that there was a hunger for this kind of theatre, Kafka being the magnet that drew the audience.

Of course, after the run had finished I waited for the telephone to ring, now as a director as well as an actor, and so felt double the frustration when silence hung in the air. I knew then that it would be wiser to choose my own material and get on with it. This I have tried to do. Like some incredible magic carpet, this production has been seen all over the world and, whether in an auditorium in Tel Aviv, Düsseldorf, Sydney, Paris, Los Angeles, London, New York or Tokyo, the audiences have laughed and been moved in the same places, and the actors have regarded it as a benchmark in their lives. As an extraordinary allegory, Kafka's short and horrifying story seems to touch everyone, performer and audience alike, and few are left unscathed by the experience. What it did for me was to allow me the scope to explore, experiment and extend my vision and, finally, to be responsible for my own creation.

Steven Berkoff

May 1995

Meditations on
Metamorphosis

October 1992

Suddenly I'm in Japan. One minute I'm in Brighton, which is sadly turning into a cesspit, although it's still charming as you run along the sea-front gulping great troughs of ozone before the white Georgian bow-fronted houses. But now I'm in Tokyo.

I slept through the night stretched out in first class. The giant jumbo jet glides over the world as we lie like those decade-long sleeps on space flights into the outer limits. You press one of the multitude of buttons and your seat grows into a bed. Businessmen are lying prone with eye-masks on and out to the world. They have eaten like fiends and now stretch out like pupae. I wake suddenly and ponder the thin skin of steel that separates us from instant death . . . no chance of survival out there. Each tremor feels as if there is a huge animal, inside the wind, whose spirit would like to heave us out of the sky. Each shake is the beginning of a movement, the climax of which would be annihilation.

We pass over the unlit world, over the dying and the new-born, over the starving in India and the killing in Pakistan, and calmly ring for the steward when our needs stimulate us into action. The service on JAL is perfect; the delicate-featured Japanese girls serve with a gentle authority which contrasts severely with those Aussie oafs on kangaroo airlines who for some peculiar reason to do with equal opportunities employ large blokes who take up what seems like fifty per cent more space than women and have to hold their stupid jackets to stop them from flapping in your food while they serve you. So this time I have opted for Japan Airlines and am not disappointed.

Susumi Matahira greets me at the airport on this, my second visit to Japan this year. He looks like a smart young executive with a touch of rock and roll, wearing standard Japanese black. He is accompanied by a pretty young assistant who has a slight flaw in one eye, which somehow adds to her uniqueness. We drive a long way to the new seaport hotel, set like an island in a wilderness of docks, cranes, factories – it looks like a reclaimed industrial site. A vast Isle of Dogs with silos, warehouses and rusting barges. We shoot up to the twenty-ninth floor; far below the motorways slither snake-like round the hotel, carrying their cargo of sleek cars, shiny-looking and smart, and even the trucks look well-ordered, with spotless fenders and their produce well strapped in. The hotel is like a well-regulated, self-supporting organism which includes a multitude of shops, cafés and even a large new theatre! This is where *Metamorphosis* will play for its four-week run. It was clever to build a theatre out here, since it guarantees a flow of traffic to the building each night and a hotel generates trade and spills over into the other arteries. Just what London's Isle of Dogs lacks – imagination, ideas and ideology. Mitsubishi, who have built the consortium, want to stage the best theatre in order to bring the Tokyo-ites out here, and that is what I am attempting to do by directing *Metamorphosis* in Japanese for the first time!

It has become a trend in Japan for huge companies to build theatres which perform as a kind of status symbol and are tax-exempt if they are part of a vast complex. Thus the industrial giants vie with each other to see who can bring in the best theatrical goods. The Seiyo Theatre where we played *Salomé* earlier this year was founded by another Japanese business consortium which was determined to have both *Salomé* and *The Trial*, and in fact demanded that we bring the second play.

In the end it was a godsend, since it would have been onerous to have played just one production and have the actors rot with repetition. I have heard of large companies travelling for months with just one show and the boredom eating away at them. In Japan we were able to rehearse *The Trial* again and everybody had new or enlarged rôles from those they played in *Salomé*. I was pleased to relinquish the big part of Herod and see Alan Perrin take the reins as Joseph K. The company were refreshed and re-stimulated – and anyway if you are going halfway round the world why not demonstrate what you have? We performed both plays with great success to a Japanese audience who seemed to want to know more about Franz Kafka.

So now I am in the extremely enviable position of directing *Metamorphosis* in Japanese in a rival theatre where the criterion is the quality of the play and not its commercial viability – so that's a relief. *The Trial* has whetted their appetites for Kafka and paradoxically this capitalist beehive sees the virtue of art as good PR, soothing and gracing the lines of their companies. Here they can charm their guests at their own theatre and achieve a high profile for Mitsubishi as knights in armour defending the fair damsel of the muse! The cost is minimal in comparison to buying up the world's great art works and, unlike hanging a Van Gogh in an office where nobody sees your $50 million investment, theatre is public and has a high-quality turnover. The choice of *Metamorphosis* may suit, since it is the story of a salesman who, following a routine of clockwork regularity, eventually turns himself into a gigantic beetle. Without too much effort one could see this as an allegory for modern Japan. From the twenty-something floor of my hotel, watching the insect-like scurrying below, I feel as if the play might be apt, might even touch a few nerves.

I'm sitting in the hotel coffee shop waiting for my host, Susumi, and I'm watching two waitresses standing idle in the nearly empty café. They are almost standing to attention, doing nothing, and one occasionally closes her eyes as if she could wash us away with her eyelids for a few precious seconds of sleep, forgetfulness, or blind herself with the endless view of the café. The other stands and shifts her weight from one hip to another, trying to absorb what is going on. She turns like a lighthouse except that it is only through ninety degrees. I try not to catch her eye so she isn't aware of anyone witnessing the fact that for these moments life has absolutely no meaning. Ah, now she comes to life, since she has been given a hot dog to deliver . . .

Last night went to a party to celebrate the theatre opening. A long banqueting table bisects the entire room, laden with a mass of sea life that appears to have been caught by mistake since hardly anybody is eating it. Prawns line up like soldiers on parade . . . a whole fish the size of a tuna lies on another dish beneath which dozens of slices of its body fan out to make a pretty design. Crayfish, lobster the size of a large TV are on display. Surrounding the table are the men of Mitsubishi: about a hundred dark-haired figures in grey suits flanked by an occasional wife mill about shaking each other's hands, but there is no sign of the star, Natalie Cole, daughter of the great Nat King Cole. She has had the honour of opening the theatre. Her music is very popular in Japan, as is almost anything and everything Western in this once culturally isolated country. For a while Japan was the gold rush for everyone who had a bit of an Arts Council grant and could cull a few faces together, but now it seems they are getting fussier and sending scouts round the world to sample the goods first before having just anyone drop their load on their nice clean shores. Saw a *Macbeth* last night imported from England which was execrable and too monstrous to be named, but I felt great sorrow for those rows upon rows of bland faces looking up in the mistaken expectation that they were seeing something special. Mind you, one can see this in London, too, this complete indifference to audiences who sit hopeful and expectant, washed, parked, baby-sitters hired, booked, planned and eventually bored.

I tend to find the subsidized theatre the worst offender since the obligation to qualify for their yearly gift from the Treasury is apt to turn what was once an ideological venture into something resembling an assembly line, which causes them to foist onto the public work that has not been tried out. It is my belief that what is shown must be the best and, like a manufactured product, subject to tests before being put on the market. State theatres are demanding that the public subsidize them once with their money and again with their patience. The old method of touring becomes impossible, not only because of the complexity of modern sets, but because actors are often in other plays in the company's repertoire and are not available to tour. With the old tried and tested method of putting a play on the road many plays would never have seen the light of day on the London stage.

Not so with my new masters, Mitsubishi . . . only the tested, tried, famous and best. Of course they are importers and not producers and it is easier to buy than to make. However, the next show will be the Philip Glass/Robert Wilson opera *Einstein on the Beach*, which is at the moment on its world tour. I seem to have heard of this show for ever, with its slightly pretentious title betokening significant insights and vision, combining innocence with profound genius. Glass and Wilson are staying at this hotel, so maybe we will meet at last. I must confess to having been a serious Glass fan ever since I first heard his powerful and moving piece *The Photographer*, about a man who took pictures of motion at the beginning of the century. You see the many stages of a man running in about forty or fifty positions. Apparently this same man committed a murder in the strangest of circumstances and the story inspired Glass to compose his work. I could hear the music over and over again with no decrease in sensation and in fact the work, repetitive as it was, grew significantly in my mind, becoming awesome and setting off many random thoughts and associations.

The President of Mitsubishi introduces himself to me with 'This is the opening tonight of my theatre', whereupon his wife swiftly adds the rejoinder '*Our* theatre . . . the company's theatre!' He hands me his card. Everyone here has cards. You do not look for a pen with which to scratch your number on the back of a matchbox. No, a crisp white card is handed to you on the instant.

Tuesday 6 October, 10 a.m.

I live in an airless fish tank at the top of this hotel. You can't even open the windows, which offer you an unmitigated view of wasteland or poisonland of endless containers, cranes and some kind of industrial chemical complex belching out a large dense white cloud of smoke. Across the bay are more railway lines, scars across the landscape and seemingly endless prongs of chimneys, strange buildings that look like warehouses or oddly shaped factories. Trucks move slowly along the dockside and this turmoil of industry goes on and on into the receding horizon until all that is left is a grey, sodden mass spiked with metal.

Last night Susumi and I, along with his assistant Yuki, had a tempura supper served in a small bar that could have doubled as a temple. Everything is perfect, quiet, and the waitress dressed in traditional robes is a model of theatrical stillness and calm. The atmosphere is conducive to harmony and peace and no doubt vital after a day on a chocked motorway and the Japanese work-style. We drink sake, a warmed rice wine, and eat endless assortments of fish while Yuki translates what Susumi doesn't pick up . . . They refuse to let me pay a penny even after giving me a huge per diem, courtesy of my agent, who wisely researched the cost of living in Japan. Although, considering my modest lifestyle, it would be no more than in London.

The monorail runs past my window and I must make a note to take this to work in future. I seem to enjoy living in a sci-fi age. This morning I try to walk along the carbon-drenched air of the motorway and I see the monorail slide its belly along the single thin track, somehow gripping it with both sides of its body like a giant centipede. As I am mavelling at it, a helicopter is zoning in to land and the trucks are crunching past me. I think of those sci-fi comics I'd devour when I was ten years old: we'd see these strange pastel mopeds ridden by helmeted young creatures through skyscrapered cityscapes whose tall stalagmites were connected by a spaghetti of interconnecting rails and the spaceships were coming in to land. It was familiar. I return to my hotel after my lovely walk along the metallic river. On my TV screen there is a message for me . . . please call No.3 for message. I explore my artificial environment downstairs. There are shops and bookshops, cafés, sushi bars, sandwich bars, restaurants and a yet-to-be-investigated sky-view lounge that is even higher than where I am by about six floors.

Wednesday 7 October

Today is the first day of rehearsal. We shall see. Something exciting about directing in another country. When visiting as a performing actor you are only a part of it, carrying your own life-support system in your company of players; the play that you are performing is your life-raft. Only the background changes, and the taste of everything. For a director, travelling is a freeing and exhilarating experience. You are in the smell of the city, alone, unfettered, swimming in your own experience without worrying about what your fellow players are doing and where shall we go today . . . Now you worry about nothing and nobody and are delightfully alone, free to encounter your own thoughts and taste the country at first hand. Also, you absorb the people, since now they are your only allies, no longer background but foreground. For over a month these people shall be my life and temporary family of which I will be the 'father figure' providing artistic nourishment and hopefully a sense of belief and identification with the work.

Start rehearsals . . . a rather quiet beginning – it gives me pleasure now to recall it since it's like the beginning of a huge book or small chapter of my life. I see him now, the representative from Mitsubishi whose organization is called Sphere, coming to welcome the actors on the first day. He makes a nice speech which is shyly delivered. Our producer Susumi says nothing. Sphere is the artistic arm of Mitsubishi or, if you like, the aftershave of the industrial giant. Tate brought me over; it is the producer and has a deal with Sphere. So there are two of them. Tate is Susumi and is my ally, so to speak. My mood is totally different here and I feel more protected and cosseted by my Japanese hosts from whom, culturally, I am half a world apart, than I did last year with my German colleagues who are really our cousins and Euro-allies.

This is my tenth *Metamorphosis* since I first dealt with the story in

1969. In 1989 I celebrated its twenty-year life in a Broadway production with Mikhail Baryshnikov. That anniversary seemed aptly served by directing it on Broadway, with the great Russian star, and I thought, this is the last time that I will direct it; after this I will put it to sleep for ever. Now it is twenty-three years old and I am not bored with it, since each time there are differences. The music, for one, is always new, no matter how arduously it was arrived at for the last production, since the music reflects the nature of the actors and each group is different. And anyway the language is usually different. I have the Japanese text written out phonetically to enable me to read it and on the opposite side I have the English text which enables me to follow what the characters are saying as if they were speaking in subtitles. It's a marvellous system and makes life a great deal easier than I would have expected; as a bonus it provides me with a Japanese lesson at the same time.

They don't seem to possess a repertory system here – the theatre has been mainly classical and the actors trained either in Kabuki or in Noh. Modern playwriting has not established roots in the country's culture and so the actors seem to gain experience wherever they can, but are not as versed or skilled in 'word play' or character interpretation as they would be in England. However, for a company thrown together, they are very good. They do have a tradition of visual theatre in Kabuki and so it will not be such a stretch for them to encompass *Metamorphosis*, which demands that the actors reflect their inner being with the gestural emphasis of the body and keep themselves in a constant state of alertness. This enables the audience to read the characters as well as hear them in order to follow the story. The mother is particularly good, even in the first days, while the father will struggle at first to keep up with the more intuitive and agile female. To show emotions in the physical language of the body seems to come more easily to women than to men. The daughter, Atsuko, seems a little stiff at first, but I can see she'll improve (and in fact she becomes a fantastic and powerful performer). Gregor is played by Amon, who has actually been studying insects in preparation; he is also a well-known theatre director and dancer, but as yet a little gauche in the rôle. He has a sweetness and ingenuousness that make Gregor appealing, but now must add the grittiness and pain.

I feel free in Japan. As if I had landed on another world with whom I have no associations, culturally, religiously or politically and nothing

I have ever learned is of any use – my tongue and language are dead, I cannot even read or write. I am totally dependent on my hosts to guide me and for some reason this helplessness frees me. I will take the best elements of the ten versions of *Metamorphosis* I have directed and compound them into a final apotheosis. Japan must see the play's zenith.

The two musicians who have been employed not to reproduce the music they heard on the tapes but to use it as a guide. Apparently they do not wish to improvise, since this is not within their province, but will faithfully reproduce what was written before. They desire specific instructions. (Eventually they do improvise and produce some of the most beautiful music I have ever had for the show.)

I begin by changing some of the choreography and for the first time strike out the multiple image I usually start with. The actors are used to coming on stage slowly, intoning the first paragraph of the story, 'As Gregor Samsa awoke one morning from a night of uneasy dreams he found himself transformed into a gigantic insect . . .' What I did was to direct the actors to find themselves, as if by accident, very close together and then back-light the image to create a single body with a multitude of arms which eerily symbolized the family as the beetle. The image also gave an impression of the Hindu god Shiva. Their collective will becomes the bug in which Gregor is trapped. Now we scrap this since it feels imposed from the outside. We give the reins to the actor. Amon begins walking slowly towards his sister, who is seated downstage in the centre of three stools. Mother and Father are seated on the outer stools some distance away, as if they were planets equidistant from each other but remote. Gregor comes centre to the first planet. He approaches slowly. I ask the female musician for a chord and she invents a long, eerie, synthesized hum that seems full of foreboding. It is perfect and I am happy today and bless those hours, and even parts of an hour, when my spirit seems to flow without distraction or disturbance but onward and inventively. In this mood I work and watch Gregor slowly enter what will be his light and begin by introducing himself. 'I'm Gregor Samsa, there's my sister Greta,' while the sister responds, 'There's my brother Gregor.' He stands above her and they suddenly take on the appearance of a brother and sister posing for one of those old sepia photographs . . . and I encourage them to change positions, holding hands or cheek to cheek, all the more to suggest those old images of our young innocence.

I encourage Amon to go slowly, more slowly than he is accustomed to, since, like the French, they rattle off the lines, revealing little of the thought processes, as if speed were some kind of virtue. Even in Japanese I sense that it is far too fast and he slows down and the sounds become richer and more coloured. I follow his words in my book. I am already learning the Japanese. 'A little slower, please.' '*Yukkuri onegai shimas.*' I suggest they speak slower than in real life, savouring the words and sounds and sloughing off the ghastly TV realism. He does it again and already he is losing that awful naturalism which suggests to me thinness and indifference. At times he acts as commentator for his character, almost as a chorus creating people for us. Demonstrating them.

I am writing this from the top floor of this hotel in hell but all is at peace after two margaritas; Yankee music is filtered through the wall of the 'executive' bar and I watch the lights twinkling away in the distance, thinking that from here I could be anywhere in the world where it is night and the uniform music of the world, disco, is swamping the atmosphere in synthetic syrup. The river winds round the base of the hotel and curls away into the distance until it reaches the sea. I am reminded of the harbour in Long Beach, California, with the twinkling lights that I viewed from a café bar in 1982. I used to go there to see my lady at the time, who was a singer. I was very proud watching her sing. She was a New Zealand girl with a lot of guts who, like many young and aspiring singers, set out to find the Californian gold and if lucky end up singing the current hits in a suburban restaurant for $60 a night. I don't know why I think of her now except the lights, music and riverside bring the image back to me. 1982 was also the time I staged *Metamorphosis* in Los Angeles with the late and lamented great actor Brad Davis, another unique artist who succumbed to the plague.

Thursday 8 October

I feel inspired. Focusing now on tiny details. It is my ambition with this, my final *Metamorph*, to stylize movement into a kind of modern Kabuki. The stage manager, who is also the assistant director, comments that flutes were used in Kabuki. I hope I can synthesize all my ideas from my previous ten productions into one and say to myself that at last the play has found its natural home, or at least a sanctuary wherein the tradition of Japan will welcome a distant cousin. I try to avoid demonstrating to the actors but it is inevitable when you have a choreographic score. They quickly absorb what I give them into their own frame of reference and since much is physical, visual and tactile, it is easier than giving complicated psychological instructions. On the first day of rehearsal, when I met the actors for the first time since our original meeting, Masumi, who is playing the father, uncharacteristically for the Japanese, threw an arm round my shoulders and slapped me on the back like an old friend. I see that he is showing that the Japanese are not so formal and are or can be 'Europeanized' . . . Masumi, who is a very well-known actor here, speaks perfect English and works a lot in America. I appreciate his warmth and desire to make me welcome and he may have thought that this is what we folks do in the West.

I have discovered that when you're 'tuned up' everything creeps in, the way a bird can down a jet by flying into its engine. So when yesterday I changed the opening for the first time, I felt liberated and ready to change more according to my feeling and insights. I am far away from the stress of Broadway and the producers for whom Mischa Baryshnikov, wonderful though he was, was the only excuse for doing a play they would normally not have crossed the road to see. Away too from the excitement of my production in Paris in 1988 with Roman Polanski. He too was wonderful, but it was unavoidable that he would be the 'centre' of the drama. And also away from myself, acting in my revival of the production at the Mermaid in London in 1986, which in fact started the ball rolling, since Polanski's manager saw the play there and recommended it to him.

But now I have clarity in the sense that all the influences that have been brought to bear over the years, of watching Kabuki, mime, the films of Kurosawa, the acting of Toshuro Mifune, of the extraordinary delicacy of line in Japanese prints, come home to roost in Japan. So in some way I return to Japan what I have taken all these years, I hope with a modicum of interest on the loan. Also my techniques are more assured and I have the advantage of communicating visually to the actors, even if I don't speak the language. I will speak the language of gesture and the body, since the first impulse comes from the body before it gets distilled, analysed and communicated into sound and thence into words. It feels very new and exciting to be directing Kafka in Japanese and yet somehow I feel forebodings here in this hotel as electronic music rolls through a kind of Nippon tubular bell sculpture in the giant restaurant. I am slowly being hypnotized by the constant sounds while the harsh sunlight is filtered through the huge white curtains, making me feel trapped in some strange unearthly paradise.

Reflecting over my new beginning I am heartened by the fact that I can still change the play after all these years. I feel brave amputating an image that was once a key to the beginning, the family beetle. The series of photographic images, as Gregor stands behind his sister, is a great improvement – it is more human. They look like a series of postcards I saw once of Kafka himself and his sister.

When Gregor begins his 'walk' showing how each day is symbolized by his travels, it is now funny. We devise a walk on the spot, a *'marche sur place'*. Now the stock in trade of every white-faced loon from the Centre Pompidou to the Venice boardwalk, it was once a beautiful movement executed by Marcel Marceau, who refined it and made it into a piece of sculpture like 'Walking Against the Wind' or his masterpiece 'The Ages of Man', in which he shows our progress through life in the walk of youth, manhood, middle age and death. Here nothing could have expressed the silent mime so beautifully and movingly. Apparently it was an exercise that the great French actor/director Jean-Louis Barrault devised with the great mime teacher Étienne deCroux. It expresses one of the many discoveries that an inventive actor can make with his body, creating illusion as if he were a physical Houdini. So Amon executes a simple walk showing his progress through the day. He becomes tired and during the walk he looks at his watch, also in rhythm, until it looks like a video playback as he repeats the gesture with exactly the same expression of horror each time at his lateness. Curiously, one gets material from every corner of the universe and the corners are usually more interesting than what is centre stage. A young black genius of a performance artist in Venice Beach, Los Angeles, taught me more about new forms of movement than anyone I know as I watched his agile and expressive body satirize modern technology.

Next Gregor welcomes his sister, who has his nightly glass of milk waiting for him. 'Glass of milk on the table, then bed, up again at 4 a.m., yes 4 a.m., to catch the 5 a.m. train, daily, what a life, what an exhausting job . . .' as was Kafka's own job in the grinding monotony of the insurance office. So Gregor drinks his milk slowly and we focus on it. He has an almost childlike quality and, as a cat concentrates its body into position to lap up its milk, so Gregor shapes himself into the right stance. Is the upraised little finger a kind of surrogate tail that gives your hand a balance as you pick up the cup or glass?

The scene progresses as Gregor recounts the agony of his day to his sister. I chose to take this 'dialogue' from Gregor's silent thoughts which occurs in the story as he lies on his back imprisoned in his carapace. I took this opening narrative and put it into the mouth of a pre-insect existence so that we could see Gregor briefly before the transformation took place – we will see him again in 'flashback' later in the play. It feels clearer to see Gregor briefly with his family. His naturalness and love for his sister give greater impact to the scene later in the play when she has to reject him. Also a glimpse of his relationship with his father:

'Did you sell much?'

'Not as much as last week.'

'Never mind, it will be better tomorrow.'

Father continues smoking, reading his newspaper, the questions to his son thrown almost casually over his shoulder, like my own father on my weekly visits to my family's small eyrie on the eighth floor of our council estate in North London. Dad would ask me questions while keeping his eyes on the TV that had claimed him as dope claims a junky. . . 'You working?' If I wasn't working I would seek in vain to answer in some positive way. Mum made the toast, pleased by the fact that I was alive and visiting. That's all I saw for years . . . the back of my dear dad's head, his balding pate while he focused on the square, electronic universe before him.

Good news! I am moving back to my old Tokyo hotel, the Seiyo, one of the great hotels in the world. I even have my old room, which seems to compress time, since I was last here with *Salomé* and *The Trial* five months ago. They have even saved some rubbish I had meant to throw away.

In the intervening months, I'd tried out *Acapulco* at the King's Head, London; contributed to the *South Bank Show* where I was able to talk of Barrault and do an excerpt from *Waiting For Godot*; completed my *Coriolanus* journal in time for publication by the Amber Press; held my first photographic exhibition; taken a short trip to the Greek Island of Skyros; and written the first draft of an East End adaptation of *Agamemnon* called *Revenge*. (And now I am back in my room at the Seiyo five months later.) In the tuned-up state necessary for direction one behaves like a surgeon in an operating theatre – one can only work in a germ-free atmosphere. So in work for those few intense weeks one has to be as single-minded as a general taking his troops to victory. The slightest germ creeping in can cause a setback.

I go for a walk and am now sitting in one of my favourite tea houses, the Lipton in the Ginza district. I just had a good work-out at the gym which is conveniently opposite and always puts me into a good mood as I watch the muscles of the young Japanese men bifurcate beneath the flesh, moving like wind through grass. Yoko, the translator, gave me a lift to the hotel. I jumped on my typewriter straightaway to deal with the latest missiles from England. So now I have the battle between clearing all channels for work or leaving a channel or two open to deal with other matters. Yoko gives me a Japanese lesson in the lounge over tea and sandwiches which never tasted better anywhere in the world. One month of this blissful, escapist existence. I loved going back to the gym and running on the treadmill until I turned into a mountain of sweat and it poured off me like snow melting. What freedom. A beautiful apartment which is my hotel with all these servants running around ready to obey my every whim, night or day. Service that is legendary, a large bed and a healthy per diem. Some work to keep me amused and a notebook to fill. Yoko to keep me company at dinner, a great book to read and no 'What's on the telly tonight'?'

Friday 9 October
Wake at 1 a.m. and read till 4 a.m. When I get to sleep eventually I sleep till 9.30 a.m. Met and taken to work by a little Japanese doll called Meguma (Meg) who admires Kafka and is sweet as candy. However, as an aside, I have been plagued by the tax man, who seems for the first time to have entered my waking day as a kind of succubus, feasting in his devilish way on my blood. I have always paid without even thinking and ne'er worrying about the tithe I naturally was expected to heave out each year, but now, because I want everything in my life to be perfect, his latest insolent demand is like a fat black fly buzzing inside my head. It is in respect of some ancient laws called 'benefits in kind', i.e. running an old beaten-up second-hand Jag, and I have been mortified by an amount that dwarfs all others. So as a worker in the theatre, whether acting as director/writer or plain

performer, you feel every demand, like blood seeping out of your being. I can understand the jockey Lester Piggott trying to hide those back-breakingly earned pounds. So different from the pound earned by companies whose families take over and allow you to sit back. Nobody can act for you or write for you. You can't pass on your skill as you can inherit a business, so it feels like a vampire has fastened his rotten teeth into my neck. Each engagement that exhausts me has no sooner been rewarded than the thing is flapping at the window again. I don't wish to live like the rock-and-rollers in Switzerland, hoarding my gold and making brief allocated visits, since I need to be totally free. So I have to grin and bear it, but for some reason now it has flooded my being like a haemorrhage. My assistant Yuki tells me about Lindsay Kemp's tour of Japan and how successful he was and I remember following Kemp to Australia. The international route seems to be available to British outcasts, and so it is fun to be a bit of an outsider, since you see more of the world than those who plough the same territory year after year.

Saturday 10 October

Yesterday arrived at the rehearsal with Meg and she teaches me the names of all the actors. I use mnemonics to remember them and I do. I think of the father, Masumi, as 'muscleman', the mother, Mari, as 'Mary', and the daughter, Atsuko, as 'let's go'. The son is Amon, 'amen', and the lodger is Yuji 'user', which in fact the character of the lodger is. My team is already there but I arrive late since I couldn't sleep and made a slow start. The rehearsal rooms are newly built and elegant and as I enter I see that there is a second-hand but bright Yamaha for sale in the foyer for 400,000 Yen (£2,000); I imagine myself riding it to rehearsal and being properly and completely integrated into Tokyo. I get astride the beast and can scarcely credit myself with being the same person who drove a Honda Goldwing 1,000 cc up the Santa Monica Freeway to direct *Metamorphosis* with Brad Davis in 1982!

Los Angeles, 1982

It was a bright blue brilliant morning and after a sweaty jog along the Venice Strip, an area of pedestrian boardwalk which edges on to the sea and winds its way down to the pier, I jumped on my sun-warmed Goldwing and take the Santa Monica Freeway to Downtown LA, where the Mark

Taper Forum is situated and where I rehearsed with my Yankee contingent. Brad Davis was a marvellously athletic and soulful young man and I liked him well. I could never forget his powerfully emotional performance in Midnight Express and when he came to audition for the beetle he confessed he was desperately keen to do it. It happens in Hollywood, you may be auditioning actors and find one who leaps out of the screen and whom you have been watching for years. Like the Woody Allen movie Purple Rose of Cairo.

I recall one moment being in a damp Victorian house in Islington surrounded by cat shit and grim corner pubs which might be models for Sartre's Hell with their nightly mantras of 'Time, please', and the next day I am whisked away to a downtown bar next to the Mark Taper Forum with one of the best actors in America. I remember those incredible 'highs' when after a good day's rehearsal I seemed to feel in love with the entire world. After rehearsal I am usually extremely docile, fulfilled, satisfied, happy and everything tastes wonderful. It was one of these nights when I was having a drink in the bar after work and I felt an extraordinary sensation of being flooded with ungovernable feelings of great contentment, as if I had reached the back wall of my well-being and could go no further. I seemed to have developed a fathomless affection for the world and everyone appeared to be endowed with sublime character-istics, even in their simplest actions. I remember the waitress seemed almost holy and inspired in her naturalness and humanity. I was gushily moved by the simplicity of her efforts, of her sweat and energy. Her raison d'être was to get decent tips and I became deeply aware of my own good fortune to be directing my own work and left a hefty tip. I remember, though, the agony of my first encounter with Met in 1969 and learning how pain turns into something quite different if you absorb it; what it pushes out of you comes from somewhere much deeper than might have been arrived at without the agony. So in this smartish bar, just as twilight settled its mauve blanket over LA, I was enamoured of the world and in my euphoric state thought that even if it should chance that I be mugged on the way home I would forgive the perpetrators, since they were only the sad victims of their nurturing or lack of it.

Brad was a muscular youth with that all-American apple-pie quality who had unfortunately a bad reputation for those twin evils, booze and drugs. Drugs and booze seem in LA to be a rite of passage that all aspiring movie actors are obliged to go through, like a Confirmation. And then they write books about their experience or give interviews detailing how they conquered those twin evils and hold themselves up as paragons of virtue: all they have done is end up where they began, but they express their adventure as if they had climbed Mount Fuji. So Brad came handicapped with a noisy tin can tied to his tail. The admin sounded a warning note about him but half liked the idea of his playing there. I was excited to have met Brad on that first day and drove back on my Goldwing after rehearsal, curiously always more nervous on the freeway in late afternoon than in the morning which, after my jog, seems like bumper-cars in a fairground. I had my earcans on and listened to Beethoven's 'Missa Solemnis' as I drove home towards the coast of Santa Monica. I felt that sheer sense of relief as the hot, smog-ridden air got cooler and I sniffed the sea breeze and just about saw the thin blue horizon as I swung my machine across Pacific Highway and headed to the home which I shared with my singer, Helen, on the boardwalk of Venice.

From the bedroom window I could see the skaters zooming along the boardwalk. One day I decided to join them, something I hadn't done since I was ten, and tried slithering along, hopelessly, out to Santa Monica pier, my legs apart like an upturned V and my bum sticking out like an orang-utan's. I was determined one day to resemble the sleek, perfectly balanced skaters with their beautiful forward motion taking twenty-yard steps while I inched my way along as if I were wearing clogs stepping in tar. I thought about Brad's audition and how this actor whom I admired so much on screen had crawled around the rehearsal room as he auditioned for the beetle and how keen he was to do it. I also recall Peter Coyote going into a strange improvisation. I secretly admired the Americans, who seemed fearlessly to reveal, expose or demonstrate their ideas and were not afraid to look foolish, since if you do not dare to look foolish you might not also dare to look great. One has to go for broke in order to win high prizes. It is not something that everyone likes to do.

As I write these notes at breakfast in my swank Japanese hotel I hear the incessant drone of those chewing-gum voices of Yankee businessmen and a woman with a giant arse arrives. Another of those seemingly mandatory attributes of the Yankee way of life. Fat-arsed Ma and Pa Ubus waddling down the street. During my constant visits to the magic town, for it was indeed magic to me, I directed plays or played in movies. I am not part of that brigade of Brits who hate LA, who never know its secrets and subculture, its remote and arcane groves and glades, its wistful mornings as the sun rises over Venice Beach and you run to the pier with the sun caressing your back and slowly walk back, melting in your own *juices and fanned by the ocean breezes. A game of paddle tennis in the free courts with my friend, the actor John Lafayette, whom I grew to know well after he played in my 1984 production of* Agamemnon, *and then the long breakfast in the open-air sidewalk café . . . some bucks in your pocket and a notebook on the table. Even the shiny ketchup bottle gleamed like liquefied rubies and with my golden eggs on my white plate and thick white coffee cup, and the blue sky and deep blue sea and yellow beach as my tricolour flag behind me, I was this side of paradise! So I would write there and each day I would write something.*

Brad died of AIDS recently, so shockingly young and talented. I remember his bright, beautiful, bouncy energy in the rôle . . . how strong he was and courageous on the bars of the scaffolding when Gregor climbed on to the ceiling. He had a lyrical, mild American twang, a kind of Midwest burr. He had rung me and said that he really wanted to play the part . . . 'I wanna do it! . . . Do you want me to do it?' . . . and I did. I was obliged to audition other actors, in the end it had to be him. He was splendid in the rôle and in the rehearsal process. He had weaned himself off drink and proved to his peer group in the Hollywood club that he was bona fide *again; with that performance he wiped the slate clean and afterwards he never stopped working, I am glad to say. So if I had some part of that I am proud, and mourn his premature passing.*

What makes the situation even sadder is that I was in LA in 1991 to direct my play Acapulco, *a docu-drama drawn from my experiences as an actor in* Rambo II, *shot in Mexico in 1985. I thought Brad would be marvellous for the rôle of Steve, naturally based on me; I asked him if he'd be interested and it seemed that he was and had some time free. I didn't actually see him, but we spoke on the phone and I rushed him the play text. His enthusiasm overcame the fact that it was being tried out for the first time in a ninety-nine-seat theatre where you worked for glory, experience and cab fare. It was the Odyssey Theatre on Sepulveda Boulevard, a worthy theatre with a good reputation for try-outs. In fact it was there, in 1986, that I had tried out my play* Kvetch *which was still playing four years later!*

These buildings are strange places in which to stage theatre. They are often derelict old warehouses or food marts that are split up like a cake into three parts in order to have three shows running at the same time for little extra cost, since the staff aren't paid, and it enables the producer to get round the law which says you may not employ actors for free in theatres seating more than ninety-nine. Well, if you have three theatres of ninety-

19

nine you have nearly a 300-hundred seater . . . so! . . . in the broiling sun you go to work and park your car and hope all the actors will be there for rehearsal and haven't suddenly had the misfortune to get paid work!

Brad received excellent notices for his performance in Metamorphosis *in 1982, although the play was unfairly compared with my play* Greek, *which had opened to very positive reviews earlier in the year. Now eight years later I was to work with Brad again, my ex-beetle. However, I had auditioned an actor called John Horne, an American whose British accent was sublime and he made me look good since he was, as he claimed, impersonating me! Brad had a slight hesitancy about one of the weeks of rehearsal and I am afraid I used his hesitancy as a lever to withdraw the offer, since I knew that Brad, being an all-American boy, would never approach the fastidious English impersonation of John Horne. I apologized and muttered excuses to Brad. (As it turned out, his presence might have saved the play from obloquy and bad reviews!) Now to withdraw an offer to an actor to play in an Equity-waiver, which is already cheap beer, is a humiliating task for a director, particularly if the actor is a friend, let alone a star. Brad was a little quiet when I spoke to him and, as they say, 'swell' about it. I asked him to come and see the play since he would recognize how rightly cast the other actor was. But he never did. I felt a tinge of remorse, and I know now that it would have been a godsend to have cast Brad since, unbeknown to me, he was already suffering with AIDS.*

The play was badly reviewed, as it turned out, especially by my once-great ally, Sylvia Drake, who couldn't handle the macho strutting. It was, after all, recording the inner tremors from the stinking guts of several volcanoes who were working on this kind of film, and these are the things men talk about when they are confined in a bar in Acapulco bored out of their minds for six weeks and working on a Rambo *movie.*

Brad died a year later. I was aghast lest he might have attributed my change of mind to a sudden knowledge of his illness. I never found out. I hope and pray he never drew that particular card. I knew nothing until I read his obituary. I was grieved that I didn't take up his offer, since it might have given him strength in his days of pain. Brad was highly respected and will always be remembered in LA for his great interpretation of Gregor Samsa.

Saturday 10 October, 7 p.m.

A better day today. I am pleased to have started by cutting that ghastly multiple image that has stayed with the show since 1969. The next image I wish to extirpate is when Gregor is doing his mimed 'daily walk' routine. The family call and act out what Gregor means to them, so during his mechanical toil we hear the sister say, 'Gregor' while the mother responds, 'Shoes! "Gregor" . . . Cash! "Gregor" . . . Cigars! "Gregor" . . . Clothes!' etc. The image is of a unity with the sister calling his name and the mother using the word to create an action that goes with the word. The trouble is that Mari and Atsuko do it so well that they make it work and Mari changes position with each word like a series of sculptures, so I decide to keep it!

The next scene, when Gregor talks to his sister who has waited for him, is accompanied by the slow-moving figures of Mr and Mrs Samsa. Their activities are performed in sculptural freezes to the accompaniment of a metronome, indicating that their lives are dominated by their domestic habits, as regular as clockwork. So now I am refining each scene and stripping away anything that is showing woodworm. In the scene when the chief clerk suddenly appears to ask about Gregor's absence from his duties, the family group wait anxiously outside Gregor's bedroom, now like a writhing centipede of flesh rather than the neat two-a-side image I had before. As the chief clerk struggles to look through the keyhole they cling to each other's backs, each desperate for a glimpse into the hole that may lead to discovering the mystery of his absence. It is more powerful, more organic and less organized.

Today I even cut my favourite bit of biz. I used to have a rather 'clever' reverse shot as the family come downstage and create an invisible door in front of the audience – it is as if we are seeing them from Gregor's point of view and the bug is the audience. We see the family in their distress hammering at the door, which is created by movement, light and the bangs of the drum. This has been a feature for years, but today I have them bang on the empty space in front of Gregor and we see a group of angry backs reminding me for a moment of the oily muscled man who used to beat the gong at the start of the J. Arthur Rank films. Their arms reach back and strike the invisible door as if it were some living thing they were punishing. So I am glad to have taken away the 'reverse' shot. It is exciting to see a new way and it revitalizes my blood. I also cut the cypher images they used to make when Gregor began to question their panic at his non-appearance. (A cypher image is when the family would create a quick mime reflection in a split second of what Gregor has said.) 'Why were they so upset?'

(image), 'Because I wouldn't get up and let the chief clerk in' (image), 'Because I was in danger of losing my job' (another image of fear with the clerk thrusting an imperious warning finger in their faces) – all cut. Now the family are frozen in their grief after a frenetic burst of activity occasioned by the insect-like squeaking from Gregor's room as he tries to pacify them. The light will dim and the focus will be returned entirely to the protagonist. After a while they are no longer Japanese, they could be European or Israeli or English. The differences seem to melt away as they did when I was directing a group of black actors in Los Angeles. After a while we are all the same and the differences are only noticeable when I see the white porridgy faces of the Europeans and Americans with their oversize bodies and weirdly Brueghel-ish mixture of physiognomies.

Amon, who plays Gregor, is a winsome, gentle and very boyish man who is famous in Japan for directing operas and musicals. He was once a well-known jazz dancer and so his flexibility and skill are beginning to tell as he contorts himself into the shape of the round, scurrying bug and climbs the scaffolding set which is his room. His face is totally open and he expresses on it everything that crosses his mind. I sense that it is easier to work with Japanese actors, as if I were moulding Plasticine. They do not appear to be stiffened by ego and status, but hurl themselves willingly and with great curiosity into the scenes, giggling at odd moments at a piece of business that they enjoy and always conveying to me their enthusiasm for the task. The parts are all equally good, equally demanding, and yet are part of a team (where, unlike a great deal of theatre, *each is dependent on the other*); they do not perform like lighthouses flashing away in isolation.

Masumi, the father, is unusually large for a Japanese; he is of mixed European and Japanese stock and has greater difficulty shaping his large frame to the demands of modern theatre. He is part of the old lighthouse-style school, but he is extraordinarily willing and his desire to learn the moves and form of the piece is without restraint. He opens himself up totally and watches carefully. Since I played the dad once I am taking Masumi a little under my wing until he can fly himself.

The daughter, Atsuko, a little firework, a ball of energy, a bat out of hell, throws herself into each scene like a fox terrier chasing its prey. Her voice perfectly captures a little girl just on the verge of changing between girlhood and womanhood. Atsuko has her own experimental theatre group and so takes to the style like a duck; she skims across the lake with consummate ease and is delightful to watch. I suppose my strange collection of metaphors for Atsuko was prompted by enthusiasm and perhaps subconscious association with Puck: 'I'll be an ounce, a cat, a pard, a bear.' Perhaps Puck was a female.

We go through a little session of explaining that the stools upon which they sit equidistant from each other are not really stools but miniature stages where their bodies 'rest' like pieces of sculpture on a dais. So they spend time adjusting and shaping their bodies to each moment as if they were craftsmen given a piece of clay to mould. Both Mari and Atsuko show their mind in their body at every stage of the events, whereas Masumi is still just sitting on a small metal stool, but he watches the others and is getting better.

The day rolls on and the minutes drip away and I try to concentrate so that I can force a better image out of myself. Outside the sun pours down over Tokyo as we work. We stop for an occasional green tea or coffee and I say in Japanese, 'Let's have a break' . . . it sounds like *Queue-kay-knee, shee-mashaw*. It seems to work, since they all stop and rush to the vending machine.

The little flower (Meguma) picks me up from the hotel each day. There seems to have been some conflict between the organizations within Mitsubishi about who should be responsible for my person, as if the two ladies were battling over me. On the other hand there could be some degree of possessive jealousy between the two, since one company, Sphere, is the overall producer for the theatre and my actual employer, Tate, is the finder. Perhaps Tate wants me to keep a distance from the larger corporation in case I get poached.

Last night went with my translator Yoko to a tiny local café which was barely the size of my hotel room and ate delicious sushi and drank ice-cold sake. A friendly wooden bar and three tables. A customer offers me some of his sake, which of course I have to accept. In spite of a malcontent spirit I am getting drunk and so we repair to another café by the railway arches. These are mainly yakitori cafés, situated outside so that the smoke from the fires can escape. It seems to form a cloud around the café and the neon from the skyscrapers blinks through the blue mist of smoking chickens. A train rumbles across the track that slices through this part of town. We order some sticks of chicken yakitori . . . A Yankee at the next table, with an upturned nose like a Harlequin and curly hair, is drunk; not sweetly in his cups but bragging to a Japanese businessman who is totally in control and speaks good English. The American keeps repeating, like a mantra, 'I work hard,' and this refrain will be heard all night from his stupid addled head. 'I work hard,' he insists, as if anyone was denying his dreary boastful claims. The alcohol has anaesthetized most of his brain, leaving him with this monosyllabic chant. Then he lifts his briefcase in order to demonstrate to the Jap how heavy is his burden.

We pay and sniff around a few more bars like ducks hugging a river bank the way they do along the Thames, chewing off bits of it from time to time. We float down alleyways until we come to a charming long wooden bar which looks like one of those places where you will always find a boozy chum to prop you up. Behind the bar is a rack of bottles of whisky, which is all they sell! We are in a karaoke bar and for about 50p you pick a tune, and your voice is enriched like whipped cream while the words float before you on the tele-prompter, but you still believe somehow that it is your voice. I dare not even begin to consider doing in public what office workers have not the slightest fear of doing, but under the persuasive influence of a whisky and Coke I attempt, and have been in fact dying to attempt, to sing an evergreen Sinatra. I even sound like Sinatra! At the end I feel I have broken yet another barrier of doing what I never in my life dreamed I would do – sing in public! I am rewarded at the end by the customary smattering of applause from the patron of the bar and the odd customer.

Two boozy tarts are having a sing-song at the end of the bar and an older guy with a girl is acquitting himself well on our left . . . there is a touch of opera here. This machine enables you to fulfil a bit of fantasy and if you have even a modicum of the talent needed, that effort will be rewarded. For all those whose work is dedicated to supporting one more brick of commerce, the chance to express themselves should be seized upon. Why should only pros be allowed to be creative and expressive? It's a strong need and desire in all of us, as natural as eating, and yet how few have the opportunity to express these feelings! For an hour or two we are Lennons, Sinatras and whoever else, from Diana Ross to Nina Simone, and everyone has the ability within them. I think half the world's sickness comes from the sheer lack of creative outlet. I recall watching the long-serving prisoners in Wormwood Scrubs performing my play *East* and seeing how obsessed they became with their rôles and how much they were putting their whole beings into it as if this was now a stronger goal and a greater challenge to their being. I pick up the mike, put down the cigarette, swig another drink, watch the words coming up and the monitor indicating when I should sing. You let it go and all the inhibition with it. I get home at 1 a.m. and wake at 5.30, read and breakfast at seven and write for two hours.

Sunday 11 October

Yesterday I read, worked, studied Japanese. We run through the beginning and it looks good and they pick it up surprisingly fast. These are very good actors and the mother and daughter are certainly among the best I have worked with in these parts. Curiously, the mother is nearly always excellent and it prompts the thought that women have certain characteristics and emotions that are brought out in particular rôles in the theatre, since theatre itself conforms to certain archetypes. Perhaps there are as many differing personality types as there are, for instance, breeds of dog. Perhaps a couple of dozen different archetypes and no more, and these dominate. Unique individuals may have a strain of two archetypes fighting for ascendancy, so by virtue of the theatre I am able to see performers fit themselves into certain patterns all over the world. It astonishes me to see that people are far less individual than they think they are, since they conform to patterns, and it is the smallest details of difference that make us attractive to our loved ones, who think we are so unusual. Mari is curiously like the excellent French actress who played the mother in my Paris production. Her movements, her reactions, her emotional responses are such that one might have thought that she had understudied her. Her way of dealing with me, her charm and her ease in slipping into the rôle, under the skin as if she were trying on a costume, are the same fit but in this case it's an emotional fit.

I think the success of performers is in fitting into the existing archetype and thereby reassuring the public, e.g. the antic boozing Celtic actor, the English suave, the Brooklyn hood, the De Niro, the Richard Harris, the George Sanders, the Jeremy Irons. Archetypes that do not stray too much from the satisfying form of recognition and, having established their public persona and found it popular, congeal themselves and inhibit further growth. Olivier constantly battled with this and stretched himself beyond the stabilizing pattern, often risking the ire of the critics, and the public, who adore archetypes. Establishment figures who are predictable in their work have also nurtured the archetypical image they think has been accepted. Like newly born stars arising out of gases we can see the emergence of the archetypes who never let us down in their faithful adherence to form.

An archetype can be most successful in the fine details that surround the central flow of its ideas; I am not suggesting that these actresses are anything but excellent, particularly Mari, the mother. Atsuko is less interchangeable and is unique in the part; she still conforms occasionally to a type of performer, but her type is far more rare. Her acting also breaks through archetypical stratification. She is small, short-haired, kind of cute and yet she has a bitingly powerful, quick, whippet-like quality, a type I have seen in others, but consider myself fortunate to have her in the play. She bears only shades of resemblance to Saskia Reeves, who played the rôle more soulfully in London in 1986, and is closer perhaps to Mary Rutherford, who played it with an animalistic quality in London in 1976.

The father, Masumi, our largest Mr Samsa, gives good value, a hearty 'hail fellow, well met' who is physically demonstrative and strikes me as having very clear characteristics, specially cultivating them for his work as a TV and film actor, which celebrates the burying of personality into stereotypes. In consequence he has difficulty breaking the mould and resorts at first to stiff, predictable movements and gestures, whereas the women's archetypes are more fluid, having to satisfy their own emotional needs and change and respond with tactile simplicity. The male is always satisfying the needs of his male group which demands predictable fidelity to recognizable type. I have found this with male actors all my life. The father is a strange rôle in that he appears to be a paternal archetype – bluff, arrogant, bullish, sentimental and rather stupidly predictable, and gets the laughs from the audience for his predictability. However, since I have played Mr Samsa it becomes a problem for me to direct another actor in the rôle, as it did in New York with the highly sensitive René Auberjonois, and with the actor who played the part in France, who was not at all successful. He made a brave effort but it was like watching a man who couldn't swim thrash around while others come to his rescue. In other types of productions I imagine he would be very good since he did have an emotional power. Since the father is a two-dimensional creation, I chose to go for every banality in his behaviour with an exaggeration that made his foibles manifestly 'gestures' or 'performance' . . . so rather than act out his behaviour in the predictable way the audience want, i.e. bullish, insensitive dad conflicting with delicate, artistic son, I played him as an actor 'demonstrating' his archetype comically. So I analysed his archetype in performance and realized that this is what I may do. Dissenters might say I am over the top, but what I am conscious of doing is getting rid of the vain and narcissistic rôle-playing in order to play the essence, uncamouflaged by personality quirks so beloved of the naturalistic acting school. The smug contempt that allowed Mr Samsa to be a self-satisfied and lazy oaf, self-pitying, whining, greedy, forces the actor to strike attitudes of male characteristics that society has never discouraged in the patriarch.

Genius changes as often as you change clothes and often causes deep concern. Chaplin's genius was acceptable as a perfect stereotype of the humane, lovable tramp, but when he changed horses in midstream he caused discomfort and anxiety among his public, who adored his realization of fantasies of the docile poor. As Monsieur Verdoux he was the tramp come of age with sophistication, but the monster of the film continually undercut his sinister crimes with such an absurd humour that one couldn't really take them too seriously. However, the film caused an uproar from the moral majority who had laid claims to Chaplin's personality.

Stereotyping is heavily reinforced in the family group, particularly in the United States, where deviation from the norm is seen as very alienating indeed . . . one has only to witness the appalling similarity of characters in TV soaps and family shows. The ghastly normality of the children into whom healthy greed has already been imprinted and deep frustration over the lack of coveted possessions well sympathized with. The average American TV series worships standardized behaviour and adherence to phoney family values, while something like *The Cosby Show* demonstrates that black folks is just as crazy and mixed up as white folks, but since they are black they have to show a deeper moral commitment, the breaking of which causes Pa to get real mad. Now, more than ever, in meeting our friendly Yankee cousins abroad one is struck by the cheeriness and 'Hi, have a nice day' attitude, as if to reassure that they are just as reliable as any other products packaged for TV consumption. They conform to the Mr Nice Guy image and even the notorious witch-hunts in the 1950s, when the 'Right' sought to crucify 'Commie' sympathizers, were prompted less by a fear of the great Commie takeover than by an inner disturbance that people could think in a non-stereotypical way about American society. Or that they could dare to flaunt their difference. One of the main differences about these artists was that they were not only actors and writers but also intellectuals, who challenged accepted, plastic, 'Doris Day' norms. They were different, and Hollywood was supposed to be John Wayne and musicals. The nation was hurt more than frightened and wanted their stereotypes to remain classic. Like classic Coke.

So who are the Samsa family? They could fit into a sitcom very comfortably . . . the anguished mother, on a constant note of pain, devotion and confusion; the daughter, Greta, who sides with her insect brother and is the hope of the family, exhibiting all those daughterly and sisterly qualities. She is above all sensible and caring and ambitious for a career as an artist, which will, of course, be thwarted by the nasty male, the boorish, unfeeling, lazy Mr Samsa. Greta eventually sides with father, as she decides that their only hope of sanity is to eradicate Gregor from their minds and believe that the creature is a strange thing that has invaded Gregor's body like a cancer. The father, at the end of the story, takes great pride in his daughter's growth and soon the awful shadow of Gregor is forgotten as he lies in his room gathering dust. Only Gregor seems truly an original being. I have compounded the three lodgers in the book into one character. He starts as a normal, charming, affable young man and ends greedy, selfish and repugnant. However, the family are reflections of Kafka's own family and as such they have a two-dimensional quality, but if you soften them they become like all families. However, as one critic pointed out, the book deals with the beetle's progression to death from his point of view and the family are mainly in the background, whereas in my adaptation the family are the foreground and I have sometimes lost Gregor in the background. The reality of staging *Metamorphosis* made it less likely that characters would be lost when they were being spoken about, whereas in the book Kafka merely stopped writing about them and they disappeared. Having created my family, for whom Gregor is the only topic of conversation, I started, like a painter, to bring them to life and add colour and shape. Gregor was seen through their eyes and they brought him to life by acting as a chorus for him, speaking about his needs – 'What's he doing now?' Gregor in turn would speak about them, twisting in guilt for his failure to accommodate and provide for them. Kafka's story is told from Gregor's room, and the family are naturally shadowy, heard through the partly open door which they kindly don't shut so that their son can hear the familiar sounds of their activities from a distance. Through the crack in the door the beetle is allowed to partake of the few drops of real human intercourse – the smells that waft from the dining room, the murmurs and the clinking of plates – and be tormented when the conversation turns sour as it involves the terrible inconvenience he has caused, as if he had willed it on himself! I simply reversed this process and had the bulk of the story told via the family.

Of course, literary critics and commentators tend to see the story as an allegory of the outsider, the handicapped or sick, the mentally disturbed or anyone who cannot conform to the norm acceptable to a society that is distinctly uncomfortable with damaged goods, or individuals. And Kafka was both. The beetle is a creature of detestation and fear, and the story is partly a hidden autobiography which he must have relished writing, since in some way he may have been able to confront the beast and extirpate it publicly. Another public purging, like 'the hunger artist' who starves to show how he can suffer by going without food for longer than anyone else. Eventually the public walk straight past his cage, not believing that he could go so long without eating. Much like the writer who keeps writing while no one pays any attention.

Monday 12 October

So peaceful to be up early this morning. Had an early dinner with Yoko last night. She probably doesn't know what to make of me when I get into one of my single-track thoughts, so we find a noodle bar which is so small it can't feed more than ten people. Two small areas were squared off with wooden partitions. Everything is warm, cosy, snug and smells appetizing. Menus hang down from the walls in strips of paper and there is a small wooden bar where two men are cooking and serving. I feel as if I am in a bird's nest. Yoko orders soup and along comes the biggest bowl of soup I have ever seen in my life, consisting of noodles and masses of lightly cooked vegetables of every description, especially bean sprouts.

It is simply a beautiful environment, like part of an unchanging Japan, and has been a soup kitchen for more than a century. The dishes originally came from China and have become part of Japanese culinary culture. It tastes healthy and is wonderfully filling – I only manage to get through half. We do a Japanese lesson, which has become our habit when having dinner together, since it provides a practical way of passing time without regurgitating one's old experiences. I find it highly stimulating, but by this morning I have forgotten most of it, and even the mnemonics I hook it to have withered like old ropes used to moor barges.

Only the distant past gleams with clarity, vivid with emotional colours like shining new paint and I am flying down the Santa Monica Freeway again, turning into Harbor Freeway.

Los Angeles 1982

I'm sitting astride my Honda Goldwing. The giant cliffs of Downtown loom up like a pile of uneven teeth, some tall, thin, clean, others like a pile of coins, some tapered, some chisel-edged as if a sharp splinter of flint had been hurled into the ground and you feel you could almost cut your finger on it. I park the bike and head down the corridor . . . those familiar smells of subsidized institutions where offices are always open, photographs of happy family life perched on nice old wooden desks, coffee wafting through and the chatter of last night's activity has to be exhumed publicly before the new day can officially be permitted to begin. People must be allowed to define themselves first before they are sucked into the general maw of the world and obey the universal flow. The corridors of the Mark Taper Forum are full of those black and white images of drama. The great ones stare back at you. Jason Robards and Jack Lemmon are among the heavyweights. I get into work and I am already tuned up and revved by my bike, my Mercury that has transported me safely from Venice Beach. The day is, as nearly always, blue, with just a fine dark grey edge at the horizon as smog eats its way into your body. It's like the black line that edges funeral notes.

Tuesday 13 October

I arrived yesterday in our rehearsal room, which I now no longer look forward to, but I manage to crawl in and out of the cab like a snail reluctantly leaving its shell. My assistant, the flower Meguma, chats to me about how she makes my vegetable juice from carrot, apple and cucumber. She adds a bit of lemon to stop it going brown. She used to sit outside rehearsal waiting to take messages on the telephone, as she was not bidden to watch, but it seemed such a waste that I told her to come in, and now she watches and takes notes. She has the benign, ever-smiling face of a nineteenth-century Japanese print in which the small eyes of the woman seem to disappear modestly. She has a tiny nose and very pretty hands. She is not so much beautiful as pretty in a gentle way.

I hate to start, so we waste time doing a few exercises for the hands. When we begin, we plough further through the play until we arrive at the chief clerk's entrance and exit. As in a dream, the chief clerk is already at the door while Gregor is still in bed, although the time is not yet 7 a.m. Dreams have a way of contracting space and time as if they didn't exist, since dreams have no need of them and merely compress events; in film we use slow dissolves as one image gradually fades like a ghost before others take over, or a subtitle explaining 'one year later' or a clock's hands spinning round so that the audience may experience an ersatz sensation of time passing. I believe Kafka may have dreamed something like this, of waking and not being able to move, since the oppressive weight of the universe was caving in on him and, like many of us, he found that the only real and utter freedom was in writing. We are told he had to work at the insurance office every morning investigating workers' claims. A monotonous, regulated ritual that would have intensified the source from which his exotic fantasies grew their blooms.

Manor House, London, 1955

Gregor was a salesman, as was I, travelling each day from the eighth floor of the council block where I lived – a gigantic beehive in Manor House. It was home and a welcome change from the couple of rooms my family shared in a small East End street after a failed adventure in America. My mother's head would poke round the door. 'It's twenty to eight!' My eyes tried to unglue and I'd drift in my thoughts and cling to my bed as I struggled to revive the memories of the previous night's escapade. It might be about girls, since I was of that age when the chemical floods were releasing their sexual opiates into me, a quivering teenager obsessed with desire, made even more intense by the drudgery of my daily toil. I recalled the nubile, sweet-smelling, lipsticked and vibrant flowers I plucked from various dance halls and jazz clubs and might have been worn out as I crawled into my bed at 1 or 2 a.m. I drifted down the fading memory of the experience and, loathing the idea of the tube, thought if I get up at 8 a.m. and rush I can make it. The darkness and smells of last night closed in upon me like a warm bath and I was drowning in sleep again, but once more my mother's voice, like a hook on the end of a line, attempted to fish me out of those depths. It would now be 8.15. I allowed myself a full five fat-bodied minutes more before sliding out of my pit and crawling into the little kitchen off the dining room, itself divided from the main room by a thick glass panel that allowed you to see only moving figures from the lounge without distinguishing any features. I sat at the little yellow table with the Formica top and generally found tomatoes on toast waiting for me and the Daily Mirror – Mum's reading material, since she liked doing the crossword in it each day. I couldn't bear it if Dad was still there, since he would have spread noxious-smelling Brylcreem over his few remaining hairs, look rawly shaved and powdered and be smoking a cigarette as, Cassandra-like, he contemplated investing his wages in a certain loser – me. I would eat and head off with my small briefcase containing, as often as not, a book, a paper bag of sandwiches and sundry other items; I would enter the Manor House tube and be sucked along like all the workers of the world, vacuumed into the West End and then belched out again at the end of the day.

Naturally, I would place myself near a young female to at least alleviate my journey somewhat from the hell of being crushed amongst the grey-suited clerks. If I was very lucky I might even share one of those hanging straps you cling on to when standing. We would take half a strap each and during the journey our hands would slide down until they were a heart-thumping centimetre away from each other and then even briefly touch as if by accident, and then would both pull away as if an electric shock had passed between us. Then, as the lumps of human work matter exchanged themselves at each station, the process might begin again and on the third descent might just let our two little fingers touch for a micro-second longer. Our two digits would convey all the joys and torments of the whole body. Through my little finger my whole being was a tingle of nerves and sensations. Never was sensation so acute. And dare I, yes, dare I, since our operation was so covert, even think of allowing my little finger to blatantly slide over hers, under the guise of accident of indifference, bruised and battered as we were by the morning's traffic, bodies pushing and shoving, poking and squeezing, the screeching of wheels and the emergence of stations; yet under all this our little fingers were the most live things in the whole carriage. I look away, pretend to be nonchalant and otherwise engaged in the ads for 'Speedwriting', a course for those who failed the more stringent disciplines of shorthand. I stare at the headlines of some bloke's paper in front of me while my heart is beating like a drum. As I *turn to repeat our delicate ceremony I see she has already disappeared into the maelstrom. She has removed herself from my heart, fingers and life and the gulf of people swallow her up just like another drop of water into the ocean of flesh. A small cell joins its brothers and sisters. She was pretty and imbued with that special precious and mythic beauty of a woman one has never spoken to but by whom one has been struck and, like a match, turned into flame. I might have followed her but couldn't since she got out at Oxford Circus and I was already late for Bond Street. I tried the next days and weeks to stick to the moment when I caught the train at around 8.35 a.m. at Manor House but never was able to find her again. I searched all the faces for her. Got there early sometimes and waited for half a dozen trains to pass, but she disappeared from my life, for ever.*

Tuesday 13 October, p.m.

We rehearsed yesterday till we reached the scene of trying to feed the new and transformed Gregor. The chief clerk has exited and the family are left alone with their thoughts and collective horror. The actor playing the chief clerk had been cast simply because he looks like a chief clerk, but the poor man cannot even begin to express his feelings through movement: he is as stiff as a rock. He speaks in that gruff, staccato monotone so familiar from portrayals of the Japanese military in the movies. Lamentably, he can't, like the brilliant Gary Olsen, transform himself into the living epitome of time. Gary played the part at the Mermaid in 1986, and played it as a weird, strange, English yob-stroke-comic with a medley of clerkish characteristics. With large head and unbrushed hair he was perfect (hair inspired by David Lynch's *Eraserhead*). However, here in Tokyo, our poor chief clerk seems like a fish out of water. The main section in the beginning of the play falls apart unless he invokes fear and trembling in the family, representing the sort of authority that loathes even untidiness and straying from the norm. The actor finds it difficult to suggest the sacrosanctity of time by the simple gesture of flapping his hands behind his back while speaking as if he were some kind of human clock. Or of tapping his feet impatiently as if the seconds wasted were his life-blood being measured out. The clerk consults his mimed pocket watch. These are all gestures which reduce him to the status of a mechanical human, attached like some little cog to the wheels of motion whose function will be slowed by any tardiness on his part. I am reminded of the view from my hotel room of the scurrying ants. However, we plod on.

The musicians always look vague and at the moment are providing a fairly ordinary accompaniment until they find the rhythm. They have to keep stopping to programme their synthesizer. Oh for a Larry Spivac, our New York composer, or a Mark Glentworth, our London one!

The panic that is released in the actors when they hear Gregor's voice shouting out for a little patience and then becoming indecipherable is very well done as they tear around the stage like speedboats that have lost their rudders. It takes some time to organize and we do it slowly at first, then faster and faster until it becomes very exciting. Then Gregor climbs slowly, as if trying to unlock the door with his jaws, always a very difficult action to mime. Then there is the drop down to the floor as he achieves it and the appearance of his arms just beyond the door tells the audience that he is now outside his room. The family slowly pull away in horror. This scene is the best it has ever been. They slowly, and with expressions of the utmost fear, move away from the object of revulsion. Mrs Samsa actually falls straight backwards into a faint and is conveniently caught by her husband, who is just behind her. A brilliant effect, but when it is repeated it seems to deteriorate. However, when after ten productions I have found yet another way of performing something, I am suffused with pleasure. Amon works very hard and slowly deepens his performance, though it is painful for him, with his cherubic face and open smile, to express the haunted Gregor Samsa insect. The sweat pours off his puppyish face.

The day crawls on and at one point seems to stop, which shows that even if I wish to change, recreate, invent, there is still a penalty to be paid for telling the story once again. The chief clerk again holds up proceedings and inwardly I curse all representational theatre for rendering so many actors helpless, incomplete, lacking physical imagination, so that when I need the simplest freeing of the mind or body they find it difficult. Here at least the women are good to brilliant but that is because they have been trained in other arts.

The men struggle against the years of institutionalizing, much like the poor British actors with their Oxbridge directors for whom the body is some unfortunate appendage to the voice-box. There are few physically innovative directors since Peter Brook fled those damp shores. Most actors wander from show to show, directed by some character who believes the best way to direct is talk themselves out of trouble. I then have to inherit their bad ways. Sometimes I am able to turn them into formidable presences and then the institutions who most resist my invasion of their territory grab my actors, knowing that they are special warriors. If this were not an insult, it would be regarded as a compliment.

Eventually the clock decides to budge and we try to run from the beginning . . . it isn't looking too good. Have I elaborated too much or fallen in love with my own technique? Do I embellish irrelevant detail just to give the play a change, a face-lift after ten productions?

Yoko comes early to pick me up and watches from the back of the room. We say goodnight. *O worri nee sheema shaw* – anyway, that's how it sounds to me. 'Let's finish for tonight.'

These notes are usually written at breakfast the next morning as I see the grey-suited businessmen, stuffed with papers and attaché cases, flood in. If I get in early then the beautiful room is nearly deserted and I order tea, croissants and home-made jam, with a papaya to start. The tea is served in a glass teapot so they can see when it is depleted and, without a word, noiselessly refill it.

Los Angeles 1982/Paris 1984

I recall the American actor Peter Coyote auditioning for Gregor Samsa in the Mark Taper Forum, LA. Something terribly awkward about actors auditioning, demonstrating their trust not only in front of me but in front of assistants and stage managers. We all inwardly admire the courage of some actors to expose themselves while inwardly wincing; theatre can lead you so astray, as it doesn't always have absolute defining points such as an opera singer has, or a dancer whose work is more stringently based on universally accepted techniques. So when I saw Peter Cayote being absolutely brilliant in Polanski's movie Bitter Moon, *I recalled him in 1982, and then I was drawn in a straight line to Polanski, who himself played the rôle of Gregor in 1988 in Paris. Who knows if they may have had words on the subject:*

'Oh yes, strange character, that Berkoff, I remember auditioning for him in 1983 and he said, "Be a beetle"! For fuck's sake.'

Pol: 'Oh he was a little strange, that's true, he kept it all to himself.'

These were comments Roman actually did make about me, but in the end the Paris production was very successful, and Roman was a convincing bug, as I have said. Strong, refined and thoughtful.

Perhaps we have a tendency to accuse others of our own worst faults, but I found Polanski one of the most difficult people I ever worked with;

35

difficult, too, with the other actors, sometimes harsh and judgmental, then at other times needing them and trusting them. Of course he was translating his fear, which he could never show or confess, into 'difficulties'; if you haven't been on the stage for years, you are naturally not going to be brimming with confidence. However, he is a brave and even reckless man who will overcome all difficulties to give birth to his dream. Even if we all suffer in the process. I had to salute his guts in taking on the rôle, which demands great physical effort and no small amount of courage, when he was in his mid-fifties.

I enjoyed Paris even if my French didn't improve, since the language would slide off me like water droplets rolling down the feathers of a duck. Glittering, staying for a moment in the corner, and then falling off. I spent two months there, walking down Boulevard Haussmann from my hotel. It was an area I had never really known before, with low-priced shops, boutiques selling the kind of clothing liked by Algerians, who used to swarm around on the weekends, and stalls outside the large brasseries selling delicious pancakes which they quickly fry up and then fill with whatever you desire. It was getting on for Christmas and the air was sharp and stark. A café in Paris utilizes all its space in the service of human beings; your every need is answered and cared for. At the entrance is the till, the counter and also a tabac. There is always a loo and a phone near the loo. Outside, against the wall of the cagé, the owner might set up a pancake brazier so from your cosy corner you could watch your man cooking up these wafer-thin pancakes and start to admire his skill, since you had time to let your eye wander and take things in.

When I wasn't weaving like a spider my web of a production, I might crawl inside a warm café and write. When it came near opening night I would sit in the café directly opposite the theatre so that I could enchant myself with my name up in lights. The Théâtre Gymnase, formerly the Théâtre Marie Bell, after the great French actress. An eighteenth-century building with atrocious sight-lines if you were sitting in the boxes. I crossed the wide Boulevard Haussmann, intersected by the Rue St Denis, where the most exotic, profane, obscene, bizarre-looking prostitutes would hang out; one of my pastimes was to walk down this street, which would eventually take me to the Centre Pompidou, where I would hope to catch some good mime acts. The street of whores carried on its trade as if it were not much different from the other trades that normally exist in any city. Offices, shops, cafés, all carrying on quite normally as if nothing out of the ordinary was happening. The women came in every size and shade under the sun and every flavour on earth was represented there, from giantesses in puss-in-boots, thigh-length glossy bondage to fat, motherly types whom you couldn't imagine ever attracting a customer since one's conventional idea of sex is associated with images of sexiness, prettiness, lusciousness, curvaceousness, youth, etc., but that doesn't account for the male for whom 'frailty, thy name is penis' and for some older gentleman the fantasy hard-on in the street soon cowers when faced with doors, stairs, strange room, unsavoury beds and the snap to attention required. The most ardent lover, who in the safe confines of the mind develops an almighty craving for sex, finds at the end of the journey that his 'herald' can't quite deliver the message. So, it may be that the older matronly types are not as formidable as the young, strapping viragos. So the male may still feel 'male'. The girls slunk in alleys, peeked out of corners, chattered madly together. Some looked tired, sad, too pretty to be doing this; you entertained the idea of just wishing to talk, to find out something. The redeemer started to peek out. And so strolling down this long, sordid artery one's imagination was likely to be fed in many different ways, unlike rehearsals, although those too had their moments.

Tuesday 13 October, p.m.

Oh, at last a good beginning to rehearsals. Get up at 7 a.m. and play with Japanese phrases for half an hour over breakfast; write for two hours before going to the gym for 45 mins; then take tea at Liptons with my fave 'mixed' sandwich which they prepare so delicately, and write a bit more. Meg picks me up and we get going.

We all shout 'Good morning' to each other . . . *Ohio onegai shemashta!* in that emphatic way . . . no limp 'G'mornings' here. Then we get down to it . . . the scene of clockwork marionettes when they eat breakfast while waiting for Gregor to get up is not yet crisp. I devised it as a ritual repeated each day, the familiar routine, and so taking it a degree further we symbolize the routine as mechanical, soulless eating. By breaking down the movement to the ticks of the metronome I make the family appear not only to be ruled by a clock but to become more fascinating as the elements of the body are separated and laid bare. The watch casing is taken off and we see the springs and ratchets within. Far more interesting to watch than a slavish reproduction of what those very actors have done that morning at home.

Of course some 'A' level critics will always object because of what they regard as naturalism in the book and of course they are quite right, in the sense that Kafka is so naturalistic in his detailed description, but then that is a book. To reproduce that faithfully in the theatre would dull the effect and soften the impact. One has to find a method that will allow the audience to believe that Gregor has turned into an insect and one of the methods I choose is to show the environment from which he sprang fully armoured as if, new-born, he had already the tinges of the mechanical world. I can't have a real table on stage to hide the actors and so, without food or props, our family of Samsas enact their ceremonies and tell the story, which is the most important element of the play. The units of their movement, their signature, are broken down and we are able to see the family moving as a trio, cutting their food, raising a fork, munching until in a way they are like living paintings caught by a strobe, or a clock made of human flesh.

It isn't working so well this morning, since the scene must still have more intense reality than that of sitting boringly round a real table. Today we start with the scene and I say that we should just do bits (this is still only the first week). It gets better slowly. As before, Masumi finds the co-ordination difficult but tries valiantly; Mari is perfect and shapes her body as if she were moulding and remoulding clay. Atsuko is still a small piece of energy that seems fuelled by nuclear reactors.

If the rehearsal gets tiring or boring, I like watching Mari. Her jet-black hair is swept harshly back like a raven's wing and she wears appropriate rehearsal costume, a long black dress fringed with a strip of lace over black tights that end at the ankle. Under her black dress she wears a dancer's leotard. Her nails are long, artificial and deep red ('I wore them for playing Tamara in *Titus Andronicus*'). Apparently directed by a British director, *Titus Andronicus* was for her a deeply unhappy experience. Every movement Mari makes is a small study, as if I were watching an exhibition in sculpture and if I am effusive about her it is precisely because this talent is so rare. An effortless blending of voice and body into a beautiful duet for one. I have to force myself to turn away from time to time so as not to neglect the others.

Since Atsuko is also unique I enjoy lingering for a few moments on her, too, but I must admit to real difficulty in spending too much time on Dad. In the end most of my energy goes into him, which he not only accepts with good grace but welcomes and tries to put to good use.

So I allow myself, for the sheer pleasure of it, a little swivelling of the head to drink in Mari's vision. No matter when I look she is in an attitude that gives me the precise location of her thoughts, like a weather vane telling the direction of the wind. Her lips are two fresh gouts of blood and her sharp features cut the air . . . of course, offstage she lets some of that voltage go and becomes simply a very charming lady, but once on, an extraordinary luminosity seems to pour out from her and light her up like a beacon.

Atsuko is no less fascinating to observe, with her short black hair fitting her like a cap, and her marble white face. She moves on her chair like a little scurrying mouse and yet her small throat emits a piercing voice. Perhaps the father's slowness in comparison with the women demonstrates innate ineptness in his relationship to his body compared to the women.

How singularly unaware some men are. They choose clothes that conceal rather than, as women, reveal. They disguise their paunchy bodies behind tailored flappy suits, while women wear clothes that don't allow them to cheat nearly as much. Women challenge fashion not only to reveal but to reshape, whereas men are content with the same old outfits. So the clothes fall perfectly round the lithe body of Mari. Her skirt is carried from leg to leg like a wave, while the clothes the father wears just flop round him. He looks less fit than he should be, is quick to grab a cig at the break and is finding it a literal sweat at the moment, but once he breaks through that adipose layer of bourgeois calcification that oppressive theatre has layered over, he has the will to be good. So much theatre gives actors a kind of psychic plague that they must chip away until a sensitive, sentient creature reveals itself.

We work with the drum and it's getting better. Marionette-like they perform their daily functions, content in the knowledge that life will continue its usual dull but safely predictable journey, but something is not quite right since Gregor is not at the breakfast table. The clockwork routine stops as the action freezes and they speak in a quite naturalistic tone . . . 'It's half past six . . . where's Gregor?' Their concern is highlighted by the stillness, contrasted with the robotic routine. The mother responds, 'Half past six . . . oh dear . . . perhaps the alarm clock's not gone off.' The ticking clock and their routine continue for two more beats of eight, then stop again as if the battery that rules their lives is running down and their routine becoming fractured. They stop, and Father questions Greta, 'Did you set it?' Greta responds, 'Set it? Yes . . . I set it for six o'clock.' Once more convinced that the routine that demands certain rules, like the setting of clocks, has been obeyed, they continue for a couple more rounds, but doubt is beginning to chew into their comfort and certainty and corrode the battery.

By this method I can see that the freezes of action while the actors are speaking not only work but make a stronger impact and statement than the way it was staged before, when they spoke while performing the actions. The picture is sharper and more focused, and their doubt crawls out of them like a sour smell when the clockwork lives are arrested for a moment.

They call him. 'Gregor . . . oh Gregor!' They spin round on their stools, facing upstage, and then spin back again like spools on a computer with an edgy, jerky action. It refreshes me to see the scene growing stronger than ever.

Gregor from his room announces to their pleas that he is about to get up. He uncurls like a foetus, beginning as a tight ball: stick-like feelers of the insect slowly emerge as if he were being newly hatched. Amon starts with his arms and legs folded across his body as he lies on his back and we must imagine that he is no longer human. I have always seen that an audience loves nothing better than to slough off the confining mantle of naturalism which makes them compare stage realism to their own lives which they often find wanting. They wish to delve into other areas of their imagination and if you give them a small gesture of something more abstract, such as the idea of a man as an insect, they will gladly fill in the rest themselves. It is as if their minds are hungry for exploration and suggestion and love to wander into unknown territory, and of course the dream factory in the human brain likes to think in images and parables. So while Gregor unfolds his human legs and arms, very slowly as if they were newly formed, the mind of the audience will automatically interpret the 'problem' and create the image. In other words they will 'suspend disbelief . The mind responds to symbols as if the brain were a curious animal that needed to forage and play in order to stay alive.

So Gregor unfolds from his squat, round ball but like a flower opening in a slow-motion film. First a clawed hand rises gradually from the inchoate mass, then another, as if exploring this new world. The hair-pinned legs jerk open a spasm at a time and his upturned face peeps through his open legs to the audience. Now his arms come through his legs, enabling him to hold them up while at the same time looking more creature-like. A thing on its back. He looks crooked, jagged and insect-like. The mind of the audience if willing to be part of the game, will grow fascinated, alarmed and then moved by the progress of the poor man-insect. In other words, 'Piece out our imperfections with your thoughts.' Shakespeare would be horrified if he saw how little his words were heeded today.

One is amazed not just by the impersonation, but by how close the actor gets to a certain rhythm. He makes a sudden movement which causes alarm and the audience to laugh. Now he lies still as if taking in what his feelers or arms have detected. He moves only a segment of his body. His head is no longer on a supple plastic neck. Instead it is jerky, moving in tiny motions like the minute hand on a clock. So the head implies the whole. Amon is beginning to make it work and breathe life into it and our tenth bug is coming to life as surely as the Golem of Prague, the figure made of mud who is created and has life breathed into him by the Rabbi Loew in order to find or make a defender.

As the cabbalistic process by which the Golem was conceived ignites the spiritual motor and brings inanimate material to life, so the magical and metaphysical in the theatre brings our subject to life. Artaud speaks of the Cabbala and numerology, and interestingly both Kafka's beetle and Loew's Golem were created in Prague. The strange and bitter fruit produced from the soil drenched in centuries of Jewish blood-letting, isolation and intolerance is the Jewish myth of a Frankenstein-like monster, and a noxious insect. Our legacy.

Wednesday 14 October

Day off today for some reason unbeknown to me. Take the tube to Asakasa, which I enjoy, and it's much quicker and cheaper than the cab. Adrian, the Japanese bellman, shows me the workings of the tube: I put 160 Yen into a machine which functions perfectly and the station is of course immaculate, cheerful, light, and you hardly wait a couple of moments before a train slides in. There is a timetable on the wall which gives you the exact minute each train is due. So you decide whether to catch the 10.02 or the 10.06.

I get into a spotlessly clean carriage, undecorated by graffiti, and strap-hang. I'm the only foreigner in the carriage and feel large and self-conscious. The city-dwellers use their journey as an opportunity to rest; half the occupants are already asleep, heads falling on to chests like drooping lilies. Many others are engrossed in paperbacks. The incredible order of it seems simple to attain. There is a map of the line in front of you, with an arrow lit up to show the direction you are going. As we hit each station, for the benefit of those who are half asleep, a voice on the speaker announces the station, so if you miss the station name on the platform you can see it lit up on the map, or if the tube is so crushed that you are prevented from seeing it you can be sure that it will be announced. Mind you, Tokyo had the dubious privilege of being bombed, and given that option who wouldn't prefer our art deco, dirt, wind tunnels and endless waiting, let alone dangerous tubes.

I alight at Asakasa and find the market I am looking for. The area is teeming with life and I enter the covered market through a large pagoda. The narrow avenues are open to the sky, but the stalls and small shops are all covered. Food shops, cafés selling sushi, noodles, shabu shabu, in which raw thin wafers of meat are cooked in a large pot in front of you and masses of vegetables thrown afterwards into the soup. The variety is endless and always tantalizing. The fruit seems huge – grapes larger than I have ever seen, giant green figs and other more than perfect fruit lie there for your delectation.

The simplest restaurant has a feeling that it is a cross between a small temple and a craftsman's shop. You might enter through a slatted wooden door after examining their dishes, which are recreated in plastic in a display which looks horribly like the real food. The need for verisimilitude is such that it seems more than real as it glistens with lots of gravy shining and dripping plastically over it.

I wander down the narrow lanes of the market. Like any other shopping area it is full of clothes, including kimonos; there are also candles, spices, cakes of all kinds. Earlier this year, when in Tokyo with *Salomé*, I bought a thick cotton kimono which turned out to have a fireman symbol on the outside, so I was an object of much merriment as I wandered around like a fireman disguised as a tourist or vice versa. The image on the back was striking and tempted me to buy it, but now I can't wear it unless I want to raise a few giggles.

Everything here seems endlessly inventive, traditional and a work of art. I pass a low wooden bakery where men are working furiously as they sit cross-legged facing a brick kiln where they are turning biscuits over on a metal grill. They then pass the biscuits to the next man, who dips them in what appears to be some kind of oil. He pulls them out after a few seconds. All this is done with tremendous speed and almost machine-like precision, turning the browning biscuits over with the wooden slats – the work looks boring and repetitive. And yet when I study the men's faces they appear to show nothing but the most rapt concentration and even peace. Very Zen-like.

There are lots of schoolkids in the market today and many seem to visit the large Buddhist temple which stands at the far end, as if the market has grown over the years to accommodate the needs of worshippers. I have noticed that another large temple at the end of town also has a huge outdoor market nearby, the same way that street markets grew up near theatres in London, physical food to help the body absorb spiritual food! The schoolchildren seem as abandoned as schoolkids anywhere and wear the same uniform all over Japan, so there can be no élitism of school or class, which seems very sensible and progressive.

On the tube back two schoolgirls sit opposite me giggling . . . they look like little dolls with their eyebrows perched high above their eyes, like those Japanese prints of Kabuki actresses. They talk with much animation and are at the age when everything they see that is not in their own likeness reduces them to squirms of giggles. I can't help staring at them. One girl still has those heavy, pre-pubescent, schoolgirl legs that have not yet stretched out into the sylphlike limbs of womanhood, although I have noticed there is a pronounced tendency to bandy-ness in Japan. Heavy legs looks at me and whispers to her friend, sending me up. I did the same as a youth, sparing adults nothing and jeering at everything that went beyond the plimsoll line of my normality. They giggle at my clothes, and my expression must look dour, a mask of death, the features pulled down at the mouth, twisted in upon its gnawing thoughts. And then the girl pulls a long face, mocking me uncomfortably.

This very April I was with the current Salomé, Myrium Cyr, in the same train to Asakasa and we took pictures of the sleeping passengers. Myrium and I competed self-consciously in our attempts at Japanese. Now I am alone and isolation draws me in on myself, as a picked fruit receding without outside nourishment gradually appears to feed upon itself, shrinking and growing old. As the marketplace comes to an end there sits a small bronze Buddha in the courtyard which opened out to the temple grounds. I observe that people touch it and rub it – the small metal figure is shiny from the thousands of hands that must have stroked it. Those who touch the Buddha then touch themselves where they suffer pain, believing that the faith they have will transmit a healing balm from the silent, inert figure. It is all done very unself-consciously, as if there was no one around to watch them. A lady I watch touches the knee of the Buddha and then rubs her own knee. The simplicity of the faith is very moving. I feel something in watching this ceremony; I wait until the people have gone away and then, when I am alone with the Buddha, I touch his head and pass my hand lightly over my forehead. Help the pain go away!

Thursday 15 October

The rehearsal goes well, without any significant change, and we slowly investigate the next section of the play. The father is absent today, so we work without him and get on fine. We have gone through the discovery of Gregor as beast and I have removed once and for all the old strategy of the reverse shot. I liked it once, but placing the actors back upstage, banging in fury against the real area of where Gregor is, now seems strangely refreshing. It works much better since they move away from the door, with their backs registering insurmountable horror.

Gregor enters slowly, almost piece by piece. He shudders down the ramp and in each small, percussive move the family react as if struck, almost as a reflex action, as if it were impossible for them to stay still but also impossible to move more than a step so as to keep their eyes firmly on the enemy, as you might do with a spider lest it sneak away and torment you with its hidden secrecy before you could dispose of it. Gregor comes to a halt and makes his little speech, wishing to put his clothes on, pack his samples and be off. He remains still, with only his head bobbing up and down or from side to side. He attempts to sound reasonable so as to convince the witnesses that, hideous though he may be, there is still such reason within him that they should ignore the monster and listen to the voice. It is as if you thought you were dreaming but were not too sure, in that halfway world where the dream is so horrible that even during it you hope you are dreaming and are mightily relieved upon waking to find that you actually *were* dreaming. So Gregor may be hoping to awaken from this chilling metamorphosis through the mere contemplation of the mechanics of work and office responsibilities. He even pleads to the chief clerk to 'spare his parents' . . .

Amon crawls over to the trembling figure of the chief clerk, but the side view is not as effective as the foreshortened view from the front, when arms, knees and hands concentrate into one image. However, we devise something quite extraordinary, a crab-like walk keeping the insect image facing front, and it works. Why didn't I ever think of it before? The chief clerk, frozen to the spot as if impaled, shakes; only when Gregor actually protrudes one thin, claw-like limb on to his shiny shoe does the clerk, recoiling from the touch, manage to pull himself away with an almighty effort, like a strip of metal tearing itself away from a magnet.

Gregor now turns to his mother, for after all who else do you turn to when the leaders of commerce have rejected you? Mrs Samsa remains downstage with her husband, having pulled herself out of her faint on hearing the screams of the departing chief clerk. Now she sees Gregor slowly crawling towards her and is fascinated and yet paralysed, as was the clerk. Mari, as mother, has a way of looking that conveys everything. She turns herself into a hook with her head fixing the thing as it shunts inexorably towards her. She screams for help, which snaps Mr Samsa into a mode of defence. He rushes offstage for a second to return immediately with a long bamboo cane – the one prop we use. Like most of our props it originated from the bits and pieces that are found lying around old rehearsal rooms.

Islington, 1972

One hot day when I was reviving Metamorphosis *for the first time, I had an Arts Council grant and I suddenly wondered what the hell I should do with it. The idea of getting money for nothing and then having to 'create' with it had the same effect on me as Gregor's appearance on his family. It caused me momentary paralysis. I had in the past three years staged* Metamorphosis *at the Round House,* Macbeth *at The Place Theatre, and an early version of* The Trial *at the Oval Theatre, Kennington – all without money. Instead of money we had intense will, desire, desperation and the tightly packed months of unemployment which had placed me in a rubbish dump of frustration that I would turn into methane gas. I fed off this slow-burning sump. It was a fount of strength and gave off a power like a nuclear core. I would avenge myself for every dull, stale, painful day that had nothing written in it except frustration and guilt! Though I could blame no one, since no one is obliged to employ anyone.*

So at last, after two or three years of putting my own productions

45

together, I had applied for an Arts Council grant – everyone seemed to be getting them in those far-off days of enlightened Labour government – and to my great surprise I was offered the princely sum of £4,000, exactly the amount I had asked for. I was shocked. So my current paralysis was caused by having to perform on cue with allotted times and commitments and estimated cash-flow needs! I decided, after many false starts on other material, to revive Met *and tour Britain with it. This would at least get the juices flowing again. I cast a young group of actors but hadn't yet got a mother. One day strolling along Camden Passage I chanced upon Maggie Jordan, an actress I had worked with at Nottingham Playhouse, where I had been acting out a couple of tiny rôles in a ghastly piece of history called* Thomas More, *allegedly penned by Shakespeare and a few others. I recalled seeing this aquiline-featured actress with masses of Titian-coloured hair passing me in the corridors.*

My experience in Nottingham was without question one of the worst in my life and I was very happy when it was over. Ian McKellen's star was just rising and he was playing the elder statesman, Thomas More. At weekends I would escape to my girlfriend's cottage, where she lived with her two small children; I would flop in the garden chair and be so overcome with emotion to be in natural surroundings with someone who cared for me, I could barely speak. I just came in, sat by the wooden table under the trees, drank tea and wept in relief to be among 'normals' again. So, many years later, I saw Maggie strolling through the Passage and asked her if she would like to play the mother in Met. *She swiftly read the script and decided to do it. She is one of the most gifted actors I have ever known. She was definitely in the mould of a Bernhardt or a Siddons, but had an energetic temperament which may have made others reluctant to deal with her. Terry McGinity took over my rôle as Gregor, since I felt I had to form a company and the best way to start was to tempt them with good parts and temporarily take a back seat. McGinity also had a roguish way and long red hair and was indeed a suitable 'son' to Maggie's 'mum'. This was when the sixties were lingering on into the seventies, so flares and jeans with flowers up the seam were mandatory costume. Terry had a beautiful sonorous voice and was perfect for Gregor.*

We discovered the stick then in that dusty rehearsal room in Islington, and not only the stick – there was an old beaten-up piano against the wall, and that too was brought into service. Our chief clerk, played by Tony Meyer, decided to experiment with the strings in the back of the piano, plucking it like a harp, and lo and behold there issued forth the most

46

strange and melodious sound. It was as if the play/production had found a perfect mate. The scenes were imbued with an eerie glow . . . just a nail pulled down gently on one of the strings would underline and evoke a particular mood and it created another layer we had not felt or heard before. Suddenly the play was transformed. Tony became our musician as well as our chief clerk, experimenting with melodies. Each day we would find new colours and vibrant moods. So there we were, a perfect team. An overwhelming actress with a flute-like voice for Mother, a powerful Gregor and good music.

So the old bamboo cane was put into service as some kind of giant pole that one might use in closing windows. With it Father impaled Gregor as a pin impales a butterfly, and heaved him back into his room.

With our newly formed Arts Council-funded group we toured Britain, opening at the Gulbenkian Studio in Newcastle. I took an acting back seat and played the lodger as a Harlequin clown with a half-mask. I was fond of masks in those days and originally played Titorelli in one too. I could escape and be more abandoned using a mask; indeed I think it demanded that of me. By dehumanizing, it releases bundles of non-human or animalistic energy that have no need to conform to civilizing behaviour patterns. A half-mask merges into your own face, frees your mouth and of course your voice, and seems to blend easily with the mobile part of you. Each part complements the other. When I read or hear about full masks being used by directors in 'Greek' chorus when the actors have to speak, it seems to me that the mask is misused and added only as a directorial gimmick.

Then we crept down to Cardiff, staying in a bleak caravan in a windswept field, and ended up in Brighton. During the tour I started to get frustrated, having to wait around all day in some ghastly English provincial town just to do the ten-minute part of the lodger at night; although it gave me enormous fun at the time, it left a large surplus of unused energy. I recall one night Stephen Williams, who was playing Dad, going offstage with Terry McGinity. They walked past me and commented to each other on the show: 'Went well tonight' . . . 'You were in good form', etc. I felt low, neglected and despondent as, for the sake of forming a company, I had lost or given up a great rôle that I had created. That problem was to come up again in future years. Terry played the rôle for much longer than I did and was so good in it that I hadn't really the heart to take it back. Instead I determined to find satisfaction in other rôles. Terry played Gregor on and off for about six years. On that first tour I did reclaim the part when we took the play to the little Hampstead Theatre Club; after the magnificent Round House it was a bit of a comedown to appear in what looked on the outside like a public urinal. However, we played to enthusiastic audiences and Terry played Gregor on Saturday matinées to give me a break from two bugs in one day.

The next time we did it in a proper setting was when, for a brief period, I took over the New London Theatre in Drury Lane and did three plays: East, The Fall of the House of Usher and Metamorphosis. What a season for a small company! The New London looked set up as a potential venue for us, since for some reason it had been something of a white elephant, impossible to fill because it was not in Charing Cross Road or Shaftesbury Avenue. Well, I like white elephants because people were willing to come and see us anywhere and since I believed this I was able to take on another white elephant called the Mermaid when I revived Metamorphosis with Tim Roth in 1986. In that Mermaid season I thought Tim Roth as the bug, with his sinewy, edgy style, perfectly caught the agony of Gregor's flight without falling into the trap of portraying him as a victim and coating his performance with the sugary taint of sentimentality, which is a temptation one has to resist in that rôle. I played the father, and Linda Marlowe as the mother was an altogether different kettle of fish from the other mothers I have worked with: she was able to step outside the anguished mother syndrome and portray the character as more of a fighter.

Terry McGinity had said farewell to the rôle of Gregor in 1978 and I had also said farewell to Maggie Jordan with whom, much as I admired her above all actresses, I regret I was never to work again. I was by this time 'maturing' and getting into creating quite a character rôle out of Dad with just a soupçon of Harlequin in him. I enjoyed the rôle and it satisfied me in an area I had not expected to succeed in. Playing a dad. I felt I was perpetually a son, but had to grow up. It fitted well since Terry was the son now and I his provider in a way.

We went to Australia with East on our first tour outside Europe and we were a huge success there. After a sixteen-week tour, what was I asked to direct the Australian actors in? – Metamorphosis of course!

Last night ate sushi with Susumi and his assistant Yuki in Edongi, the largest sushi house I have ever seen. Since it is situated opposite the fish market I am constantly assured how fresh the fish is. Try to keep my 'marbles' from rattling too much and be a civilized human being.

1 Steven Berkoff as Gregor Samsa,
The Round House, London, 1969.

2 Terry McGinity as Gregor Samsa,
touring production, 1976.

3a Ralph Cotterill as Gregor Samsa,
Nimrod Theatre, Sydney, 1976.

3b Asher Sarfaty as Gregor Samsa,
Haifa, Israel, 1978.

4 Brad Davis as Gregor Samsa,
Los Angeles, 1982.

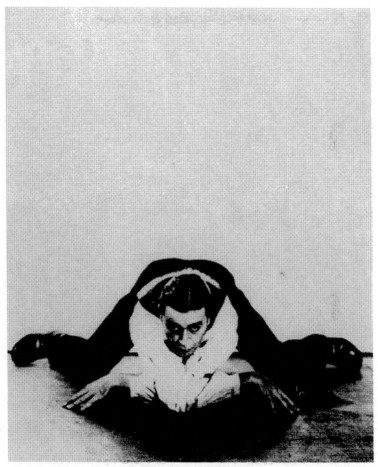

5 Bernd Jeschek as Gregor Samsa,
Düsseldorf, 1983.

6 Tim Roth as Gregor Samsa,
Mermaid Theatre, London, 1986.

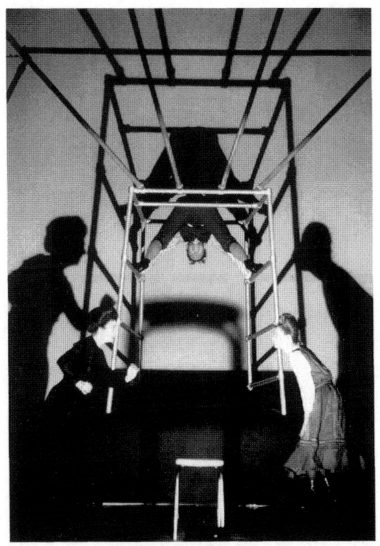

7 Roman Polanski as Gregor Samsa,
Paris, 1988.

8a Mikhail Baryshnikov as Gregor Samsa,
Broadway, 1989.

8b Amon Miyamoto as Gregor Samsa,
Mitsubishi Theatre, Tokyo, 1992.

The raw slices of fish look like tongues draped over little beds of rice and they keep coming. We speak of all the fantasy projects we wish to do. Movies of *Salomé*. A movie of *Kvetch*, a play which had won Comedy of the Year, my first major award in Britain. Since our season here with *Salomé* and *The Trial* our profile is very high in Tokyo. *Decadence* is now announced in the papers as a movie to be made in early 1993 and I haven't a clue except that Joan Collins will be in it. Susumi and I can't quite delve beneath the surface of business talk, but we are getting closer. He tells me for the first time that he has a wife and two children who live outside Tokyo and I have to imagine them. Susumi is a young-looking forty-three. With his black hair, black Italian designer suit and black shirt, he looks like a sleek black cat.

After the meal we go back to my hotel which has encased in its womb a dark 'members' bar, faced in charcoal-grey marble; it looks like the kind of place you go for intense privacy. We drank margaritas and talked about the mime/clown Lindsay Kemp whom they produced five times in Japan and who is a big star there. Of course we are always more interesting to another nation since we have things they do not have and vice versa, and so there will be a fascination merely with the differences that exist between us. We like sushi in England and America! The Japanese adore American pop and rock music. Whether or not acclaim in another nation suggests your art is great and unrecognized by the philistines at home or whether its freshness comes only from its being another flavour and therefore stimulating, only you can answer.

London, 1963

I remember Lindsay Kemp many years ago doing his shows in a little attic off St Martin's Lane called the Hovenden Theatre Club, run by a formidable old lady called Valerie Hovenden. They were very clever, pungently sweet shows devised round the character of Pierrot, who is Lindsay.

A frequent show-stopper, which he managed to find a place for in many of his shows, was a strip mime. It was the funniest piece of clowning I had seen and worthy of a Chaplin as Lindsay cavorted with his mimed bra and played with his grossly enlarged tits. He claimed he got the idea from teaching Soho strippers how to strip seductively. I'd never seen anything like Kemp and admired his ingenuity and bizarre magic. To reach the little

Hovenden Theatre you climbed three or four flights of stairs – it could have been something out of The Picture of Dorian Gray, when Dorian wanders into the fringes of London looking for his nocturnal pleasures. Lindsay was and is a weird concoction of Marceau, panto, ballet, seaside postcards and Genet.

By the time I met Lindsay I was already fascinated with the art of mime and had been studying with Claude Chagrin, the great mime teacher and disciple of Jacques Lecoq. Lindsay and I showed each other all the tricks of mime in his living room. Having moved on from the tiny Hovenden Theatre with its audience counted in dozens, he has for many years played to thousands and the Japanese seem to have taken him to their heart. Lindsay is a theatrical Marco Polo, rooting himself in one country and then tearing himself out and replanting himself in another. Once the theatrical guru of Edinburgh, which is a city well suited to him, he then took off to America, flopping on Broadway and replanting himself in the Lower East Side, performing his Salomé. He lived for a while in Barcelona, putting down roots and forming companies there, only to take off years later to replant himself in Rome. I recall his endless productions of Flowers, in which he always played the heroine. It was beyond The Valley of the Dolls and took ham so far it became a new art form, notwithstanding occasional scenes of real beauty that stunned the eye.

By this time I was staging my repertoire season at the Round House, Chalk Farm, in the exciting days of the early seventies before it was cleaned up, which was to lead to its eventual death. Lindsay and I were always a little in competition with each other and sneakily envied each other's successes. In other ways we were like old dogs burying our ancient bones and digging them up from time to time – his bone being Flowers and mine Metamorphosis. So there he was, a photo in the producer's assistant's pocket, with white face and familiar pixie grin, but instead of Harlequin it was now kabuki and onnagata.

Friday 16 October

Feel shitty this morning as I wake late (9 a.m.) and drag myself into the breakfast room, where for an hour I am treated like some minor royalty – my tea is replaced after I have half drunk it and a waiter attends every gesture or movement of my head, ready to fulfil any whim I might have. But I feel like death, so I grab a brolly from Adrian the porter, and walk to the gym. Spend twenty minutes on the treadmill until my body's fluids are exploding out of me. Do some bench press, some squats and feel considerably lighter in spirit and body; go to rehearsal still sweating and we take it from the stick, when Dad impales Gregor as he shoos him back into his room. Now, whether through the gym or not, I find a far better way to perform the scene and actually add a special movement to it.

The way I have usually staged it is for the father to aim the long stick at the prone Gregor and by catching it under his belly appear to lift him, although the actor playing the beetle is doing most of the work himself, using his legs to half stand. I then used to freeze the action while the two actors stepped out of the story to do their own narration. This was effective as a jolt to the audience, since the actors' bodies were in an attitude of extreme tension while their voices took on the tone of the dispassionate observer. Gregor, in his exposed belly position, said, 'Gregor was quite unpractised in walking backwards and was afraid to annoy his father any further the time it took to perform these exertions . . .' Then Mr Samsa took over, adding, 'His father, for his part, had no intention of making things any easier for Gregor by opening the door, but merely wanted him out of the room as soon as possible.' There is no easy way to render this narrative in the first person so demanded of 'stage dialogue' and naturalism. In a lot of plays it would be dropped since it has no function there, and a valuable piece of thought would be lost. However, it can and should be included by changing the action. This allows the actor to switch 'modes' and go from acting to commenting.

But today, rather than having Gregor lift his body on to its legs, I have the father bang the floor left and then right . . . We watch the beetle move suddenly and defensively, which is a sharper movement, and then Gregor crawls back by stages into his room. As he is about to retreat to safety, Mr Samsa raises the stick like a spear as if to impale him, then they freeze and narrate. So the action is frozen while their other halves speak, *then* the play continues with the father about to bring the spear-like stick down. Just before he can wound Gregor the daughter and wife rush in and grab the two ends. They freeze as if in a frame of film, as if their lives were fixed forever in their eternal struggle with this absurd stick, one at either end. As if the stick has become an extension of the father, like a pair of horns that the women are holding on to, trying to prevent the dominant male from inflicting any more woe.

I view the father as naturally aggressive. We take from life and my research over many years into the strange habits of fathers has led me to view them as aggressive by instinct. I am wary of them as one might be wary of a dangerous animal.

After a second of revealing this 'image' of their struggle, they move, circling, but the father wrests the stick from the two women and having expended his fury thinks better of wounding Gregor and throws the stick offstage. They collapse into each other's arms, for once united in their inconsolable grief, and Mr Samsa now needs the comforting reassurance of his wife and daughter. He almost appears to crumble after the event, as if fouled in his spirit in recognition of the fact that he could have cruelly damaged the unfortunate insect form of Gregor. The women are relieved that Mr Samsa's fire is out and they also have their own need to unite. The rehearsal continues to go well and new effects are being produced throughout the day. At 5.45 p.m. we pack up, saying *Otskarete sama deshta* the usual expression at the end of rehearsal, 'Have a nice evening.'

Saturday 17 October
Sleep well and watch the presidential debates on the TV. Aghast at the sluggishness of the Bush/Quayle, Batman and Robin duo. Quayle comes across as such a repellent little turd. I believe actors have such a trained eye to interpret body language in their work that they notice immediately, or at least I do, when the body or inflection lies. Quayle seems a phoney to his fingertips. The Democrat's voice and body language come across as sincere, authoritative, and make a strong impression of his belief in what he is saying. When Clinton, or his deputy rather, is speaking, Quayle grins rather than listening soberly to his opponent's arguments before trying to demolish them. The snickering and grinning while the opposition is making his speech are a typical weak demonstration of 'upstaging' your opponent. The smile also covers the fairly obvious fact that you are burning inside with anger but pretending it's all goofy. So you are lying to yourself. Quayle behaves like a school wimp snitching on his friend . . . 'You're not telling the truth,' he squeals; a pathetic, snivelling accusation from someone who worked for the biggest fraud in history.

I don't really recall when I came across *Metamorphosis* for the first time, but have a feeling it was in an American army base in Bitburg in Germany during my stint out there as a salesman for Burberry's gentlemen's outfitters. The American stores, which were gigantic and fed the collected families of the US Forces in Germany, used to let out or give concessions to foreign products which they thought were 'quality' items, and so the famous house of Burberry's let its name be used and its label was sewn inside suits and jackets that even I knew had as much to do with Burberry's as the man in the moon. The finish was often shoddy and it would take an unfathomable eight weeks to come back from whatever London sweatshop made them up. There were no fittings, since not only would there not be time, but the jerks working there wouldn't have a clue how to 'fit' or alter. So the suits sometimes came back looking very strange. However there would be a local alteration tailor at hand to re-hack them into shape and take in the cavernous waists. (They all came back several sizes too large since it was thought that you could at least take them in, but if they were too small then you had had it.) I half enjoyed and half hated the little cubicle, but found it rather fascinating at the same time and, thrill of thrills, you could use the military PX snack bar!! There I could re-indulge in all those Yankee foods that left such a taste of nostalgia on my lips since my aborted immigration there when, at the age of ten, I embarked with my family on the boat to the USA, only to return to England three months later – a shock I don't think I ever recovered from.

I spent a lonely Christmas in Bitburg – so much for the generosity of my colleagues; however, in the well-stocked library, among other facilities on the base, I found solace and Franz Kafka. I liked the American books with their large formats and plastic covers; they looked serious and were full of sci-fi. I was exploring the shelves when I came across this strange-sounding name and was drawn to it. Kakfa. Now what on earth was that? I took out *Metamorphosis and Other Stories*. The curious thing was that nobody introduced me to Kakfa. I discovered him by accident, as if led to him by some metaphysical agent. These were simply beautifully written tales with which I identified and found myself in accordance, though for what reason I could not quite fathom. Perhaps it was the innate simplicity of recording the nervous system of the human beast. I developed a taste for the exotic and bizarre. Eventually when I decided to direct my own works I tried to pull a play from it and made up one of sorts, but, untutored as I was in the alchemical possibilities of the stage, I could not 'see' the insect appearing and so made the family the focus for seeing it. We saw the creature through their eyes as if, as in a Greek play, the tragedy happened offstage. In the story, the tale is told by

Gregor reporting on his family from his room to us. However, in the play I reversed it since I could not see how on stage the beetle could do this. I had the family telling the story simply by giving them Gregor's lines. In the original Gregor complains about feeling thin or weak; I had the sister reporting on how thin he has become. When in the story the family are seen talking about investments, I had them enacting a whole scene with Gregor listening in. So by taking the opposite approach to Kakfa's I still portrayed the situation largely as Gregor saw it from his room.

In order to stage this I had the family seated downstage on three stools, equidistant along the base of a triangle, while Gregor reclined on a platform upstage centre as the apex. The family performed the usual functions, heard and watched from his room by the insect, who was allowed a little crack of the door left open. So the family reflecting the bug became overwhelmingly important as they reported progress, while Gregor was increasingly ignored until he gave up the ghost. At the same time this approach focused on the family's agony and plight in dealing with the tragedy. Father, mother and daughter became fleshed out and as vital in their own way as any Chekhovian characters. They went through their own metamorphosis, and with his death they were somehow reunited and restored to normal life – their last words expressed concern not about Gregor but about finding a good husband for the daughter, Greta. No sooner does Gregor die than his life becomes a mere shadow that passed over them; that is the power of the story. It is not a particularly complex tale, but extraordinarily descriptive; the daily minutiae of their lives are tellingly recorded with precise detail. The Samsas are an average, ordinary family with ordinary, simple, human dimensions. Decent, hard-working, proud.

In the early days when I took the rôle of the father, I found it difficult, since I felt myself always to be a 'son'. I last played Gregor in 1972, when I was already thirty-five, with Stephen Williams, albeit younger than I was, playing my father. Eventually I wanted to get off my knees, out of that cramped position and walk again, stroll and act as a human being. It came about when I was rehearsing *Met*'s first revival, with Matthew Scurfield playing Dad. The rehearsals weren't going well and we decided to change parts. Terry McGinity took over the part of Gregor, which we had shared earlier, and I stepped for the first time into the part of Father. Matthew played a very funny lodger and I struggled with maturity, playing a dad for the first time in my life. I imagined all the fathers I had ever known, starting with my own. I saw old photos of my grandfather from Russia and decided that the short, squat, powerful body, the paunchy belly, the belt inches down the waist and the trousers tucked inside the socks was the image I wanted. A stocky Russian peasant, sitting, knees spread wide, vulgar, a walk with the bum jutting out as if he still had barrels of pickles on his back. A strong, grizzly, working-class peasant. It seemed to fit and I mixed some flavouring from other stray characters: a bit of comedian Les Dawson, Olivier, an end-of-pier comic, plus a bit of clowning. He was in danger of becoming a mite too comic, a parody. I had to be careful that I was not competing for attention, having relinquished the showier part, but I was determined to demonstrate the potential of Mr Samsa.

I was younger then and still living off the soup of frustration deep in my craw. I had created the whole production, but the motive behind it all, the driving force, had been my desire to show this monster/creature/human and express the versatility that conventional theatre could never accommodate. I wanted to demonstrate the ideas that are open to us when we eschew the plaintive whine of naturalism, worrying about getting old, the orchard being chopped down, being left on the shelf. So since my overwhelming desire was to detonate all other forms and delineate the segments of the body, create an illusion on a par with Houdini, it was a bit galling then to have to play a mere *human*. In consequence, I decided Mr Samsa would be a human cartoon, part marionette, a parody of all father figures, authoritarians. This scheme worked for the mother and the daughter as well. But I knew that the great question mark that hung over the audience's minds would be, 'How on earth will he play the bug?' not, 'How does Berkoff play the father?'

I prided myself on being able to speak and move, and on the fact that I had taken the actor's body as seriously as his voice, mind and totality of his equipment. My metamorphosis was *my metamorphosis* from common under-employed actor to entrepreneur, director, actor, writer, mime, all rolled into one fist – one giant ball that would shatter the plate-glass window of British theatre. Largely it did, when we opened our first production of *Met* in July 1969 at the Round House.

It was a scorching hot summer and all the theatres were flopping like flies. But after a strong review from the late Harold Hobson we rallied. Hobson mentioned the performance in the same breath as

Henry Irving, comparing our abilities to astonish an audience, he
playing Mathias in *The Bells* and I playing Gregor Samsa. What an
accolade! And so for the final week we were sold out. We were what
people wanted from the theatre and even in the heatwave in the hot
Round House they flocked.

I was very proud and always remember playing there. I liked the set
made of steel scaffold resembling a giant insect. I would lie on my back
and recall the papier mâché and soft canvas in Dundee and Perth.
Now my hands felt right as they gripped the cool steel, and as I
climbed the frame and hung upside down from the centre of the metal
canopy I felt truly in my element. I was thirty-one and yet not so fit,
since after three weeks I was exhausted. Performing the curtain-raiser
didn't help, as it was practically a monologue based on Kafka's short
story 'In The Penal Colony', in which I played an officer who, unable
to convince a visitor of the beauty of capital punishment, climbs into
the machine and executes himself. In a rare lapse, Harold Hobson
misunderstood the piece and imagined Kafka enjoying the sadistic
torture he wrote of so vividly. This rather dampened the euphoria of
the second part of the review. However, I chose to ignore his
shortcoming on 'Penal Colony', believing that he had found his senses
for the main bill.

George Hoskins was my mentor at the Round House and his
encouragement and visible affection made me want to do more and
perform there again. He was an odd chap whose cupid lips and long
silver hair gave him the air of some eighteenth-century decadent. He
ran a fascinating theatre and welcomed the bizarre of the world – why
compete with either the Barbican or Shaftesbury Avenue? Then
others took over the running of the building; in an article for a
magazine the new administrator was interviewed and said that it
wasn't a pretty sight when it was taken over – there were syringes in
the toilets! Now there are no syringes since there is no theatre. There
must have been money problems inherent in such an unwieldy site,
but it was a magnificent building and I am sure George wouldn't have
let it die. George Hoskins imported the world of theatre: the Open
Theatre of New York, the Living Theatre, the French Magic Circus,
Kemp, me, and all those awful groups who were too naughty to be
given house space in today's antiseptic mausoleums.

We had a gigantic poster on the front of the building which Alison
Minto, who became my wife, conceived. The cast all had a deep

enthusiasm for the play and we rowed heavily only once, when I invented a piece of business after the beetle has returned to his room. George Little, playing the father, criticised it severely and said you couldn't have another event after the opening climax. I loved my multiple image, but on reflection he was right. We had climaxed and all it needed now was a calm reflection of the event. George was certainly the best Mr Samsa we ever had and I learned from him, although my performance was completely different. He was a strange bloke who insisted on warming the cups before we had tea. In this, like many other things, he was right. Jeannie James, who played the mother, eventually turned to painting, although she was a strong, fiery actress, and Greta was perfectly played by Petra Markham. I recruited an able administrator by the name of Christopher Munke whom I had taught at Webber-Douglas. So I had my first team.

Sunday 18 October

Breakfast. Feel much better this morning although I haven't worked out the reason. Last night went with Yoko to a restaurant where they cook the food in front of you on huge silver metal hotplates. It is a form of entertainment as you eagerly await your treat being sliced up live in front of you. The restaurant is situated in a modern hotel in Asakasa and we sit at a horseshoe bar and watch the proceedings as if the bar were the stage where sundry performers would make their sacrifices. Not so much the hot seat as the hot plate!

We order beer and the set meal for 12,000 Yen. Sixty pounds! You can eat really well in Japan for a fiver, actually, especially in those self-service mini-railway cafés where the food comes along on a conveyor-belt and you grab it and pay by the plate. It's rather Chaplinesque and reminds me of *Modern Times* – just speed up the conveyor-belt with its little plate of sushi and you have the makings of a comedy. Once you get to high-tech surroundings the prices leap to dizzying heights. We opt for a filet mignon. We are served a salad nicely seasoned and a little bowl with some creature's innards shredded up.

At home I always knew exactly what I was eating; Mum would cook fish cakes made from haddock and cod chopped together. An occasional kipper, and certainly rollmops were a fave, perhaps chopped herring; smoked sprat spread on rye bread was a treat. You knew and saw, there were no creatures whose form was unidentifiable and bizzarre with tentacles, proboscis, feelers and squidgy bits. Mum's cooking was simple but extremely tasty. You ate the flesh and not the organs, you did not boil things alive, nor pull living things out of shells.

The mignon comes out looking like a little red brick with a layer of cement clinging to the surface. The cook sets it on the griddle in front of us while he prepares our bean sprouts. The steak is choicely undercooked, then he chops it into small cubes, which I don't think is such a good idea as it will quickly lose its heat. We are given a small dish with three sauces and we dip our chunks of meat into them. The chef sizzles up one of our filets at a time and we share the first, knowing, with some degree of satisfaction, that another is on the way.

I examine the crowd . . . two Englishmen, or Aussies more like it, sit with huge paunches before them and look very much the worse for wear in the obsessive pursuit of financial rewards. One is especially fat and as he moves he knocks a jug of soya sauce which falls over and spills everywhere. He is contrite and apologizes to me in case some splashes found their way in my direction. I suddenly feel for the pain that all that fat represents and choose to respond as if it has almost been a pleasure. Opposite us on the horseshoe bar a group of Americans come and look solemn, as if the meal is to be taken deadly seriously, so they must be foodies. Yoko and I chat about God knows what – it is one of those evenings when a clamp is shut on my reveries and so I recycle the junk that hangs around outside the door of my inspiration.

There is a second and more expensive menu, the same as ours with the addition of crayfish, which the fat men are having. We enjoy the steak and Yoko, in her wonderfully indomitable Japanese fashion, tries to entertain me as if she were the captain of a ship guiding it through a momentary squall. Although working only part-time, she refuses when we go out to let me pay for anything and so I have to get my wallet out fast when she is with me.

After the sizzling steaks the next performance is to be the live contestants, who give us some form of entertainment the prone steaks cannot provide – although the chef with his tall hat, immobile features and hands like the scything legs of a ballet dancer attacks with his knives like a master surgeon of the kitchen. On a dish which looks as if it has just been taken out of a fridge are a few crayfish, like rather large prawns, which have been denuded of the lower coat of their shells and wear a top half, so they look as if they are naked apart from a small bolero jacket.

As I watch the half-naked creature whose shell was no doubt painfully torn off, I see it move! It moves again and I see that it is alive! Yuk, I think, and ye gods. It is lying live on a plate, stripped of the dignity of its life, waiting to be put directly on to a hotplate. Its raw flesh exposed to the burning iron. I can't really believe it. Don't the customers or the chef realize it's live? It feels. It senses. Or do they think it's somehow like an animal/vegetable, some hybrid, or don't they in fact care? Or is greed so overwhelming that it precludes any sensitivity or awareness for the pain or discomfort of others? I like a creature well dead before I eat it. I try to imagine that the crayfish has been in the fridge some time and is dozy or numb and its reactions are simple reflex action. It could, on the other hand and more likely, have just been pulled out of a tank. So it moves a little . . . so what? The audience, apart from me, are paying scant attention to what to me is the small-scale equivalent of watching someone go to the electric chair.

So the time comes for the fat man's starter – crayfish is for him. The chef, meanwhile, seeing me eye the moving creature, has delicately covered the group of shellfish with a bowl to spare us their dying throes. Now he lifts the lid, swiftly placed the four on the hotplate and pressed a wide spatula over them . . . The 'live' one reacted to this new atrocity and weakly beat its tail in protest against the hotplate . . . I had no doubt that the thing was still a being with life, sensibility and pain. The sight actually fascinated the young American woman opposite whose face suggested that she found it not altogether edifying either. It was living and being fried live. They could have chopped its head off first . . . there was no real need to place its live tissue against a burning grill. Its agony, if it still could feel, lasted several seconds, for even as the chef again pressed his metal square on it the small creature still refused to abnegate its life. Now the chef seemed a touch annoyed with it and this time, as he lifted his spatula off, he took a sharply pointed knife and pulled rather than cut the heads off, which he then threw into a hole in the grill, no doubt to be used for soup. Everything in the end is just cells and blocks of protein . . . it's what they become that changes our view of civilization and how we perceive them that makes us human. If not, we too are just cells, meat, atomic particles. The crayfish were then split in the middle, twisted up and served . . . in the end it didn't look as if it was worth eating.

Then for the next delight of the evening, after I have eaten my steak, an abalone is ordered and out comes this large shell with, of course, a live mollusc happily ensconced inside its home. Naturally it must be live, since shellfish have a tendency to go off very fast. This creature's thin outer lips are moving very slightly, so what will happen now? Will he kill it in front of us for our delectation, cook it? Predictably the soft abalone, used to the delicate embraces of water and the soft undulations of the waves in its salty sea home, now finds itself placed face down on the hotplate until it sizzles. I see the shell moving slowly on top of it until it dies. Then the chef lifts the shell and removes the curious assortment of shapes and organs. There is still evidence of a current of life running through it. He then slices it in two – one half looks like an upturned mushroom. However, this does look closer to the vegetable or plant world than its predecessor. Yoko pays and we leave. She says in the cab going back to Ginza that she has never noticed those things before, although she may have said this to alleviate any embarrassment I may have had dealing with my Western squeamishness.

Hated going to work yesterday, although I have barely begun. I always hate going in. I remember simply loathing the beginning of the day in the Public Theater, New York, when I was directing *Coriolanus* for the first time. Perhaps, as I look back, it is because I know that each day is going to be a fearsome expenditure of energy and that I will try to lock horns with inspiration; somehow my body senses that all this battering is to come and is reluctant to step through the door. However, after I have got into it, there are times when I can't bear to leave it. I loved the end of rehearsals in New York when I would step out into the sharp, biting air after directing Mischa Baryshnikov in the New York *Metamorphosis*. However, I don't recall it as clearly as *Coriolanus*. It seems to have faded into a misty series of images. But I always recall the smell of Lower Broadway. Going down in the lift, Mischa with a funny beret on, placing his thin wrist watch to one side when he started rehearsing. And how proud, how very, very proud I was to be directing this most fantastic of animals in a rôle which needed movement – I was actually showing Baryshnikov the moves! For me this was the peak of my achievement. Demonstrating choreography to one of the greatest movers who ever lived . . . I have never lost the sensation of that feeling. And so it is hard to remember other things so well, even if I do recall the splendid acting of Laura Esterman and the difficulty the excellent actor René

Auberjonois had playing the father because I kept trying to carve it in my image, which was the parody father, all bluster and bullying, the cardboard cut-out. René was not so much of a satirist but a brilliant, serpentine actor and I think he felt sometimes that the rôle didn't fit, but in the end he was superb. I felt sorry for Mischa having to obey the strictly boring Broadway/West End work ethic of eight shows a week. It must have killed him emotionally and turned something that might have been rewarding into a nightmare.

Meanwhile back in Tokyo. We have to change our rehearsal room since the better and larger basement has been booked by the cast of a musical who thump their music all through our rehearsal; at times I don't know if it is our musicians or theirs and sometimes there is a weird mix from the two groups, which leads me to believe that our lot are doing something pleasantly inventive until the truth dawns on me. The chief clerk is worse than ever and I try to resist the desire to use the poor man to purge myself of the bile which is the accumulation of ten revivals. When this production works it is wonderful, but if an actor is miscast and can't express himself in his body, it is an onerous and troubling time.

I had a thought just now about the actors I see coming to me for auditions. Some are very good, but most are wretchedly unaware of the totality of their being and are awkward, deprived of *artistic nourishment* and under par. I can only compare it to a doctor going to some rural area or foreign country and finding the people suffering from malnutrition because they are not getting the vital vitamins to make them whole human beings. In London even more than in the USA, I find this poor specimen of an actor undernourished unless he has played substantial parts, a victim of the status quo director whose belief in spurious impersonation drives the player into creating simple character studies with loud voices and no colour. A victim of stage blood, dry ice and choreographed fights.

We continue trying to get the chief clerk to think with his body and not just say the words parrot-like with a bit of 'anger'; to express the insane panic of the clerk in his body, which even moves like a ticking clock. Alas, the poor player has been prostituted for too long and is too old, but he tries.

Monday 19 October

Like Joseph K, I have to work today but don't feel like it with one of the cast missing again, the unfortunate Masumi who plays Dad. He is improving, though. Again the Dad problem. Probably if I had played Mum there would be a problem with all the Mums. There are too many people around anyway. A sound technician, two musicians, a translator, a stage manager, an assistant director, a girl who sits and writes and brings me fruit juice. Two people from the Sphere company watching proceedings on behalf of their bosses. Plus the cast, and apart from Dad everything seems to go smoothly. We have a marvellous eruption when Gregor suddenly appears in the room. A twitching, fast, screaming family explode out from the centre like a bomb and then freeze into silence. It's wonderful and expressionistic . . . the effect on the audience is to chill, to stun and make them aware. We keep improving on the old model all the time.

The next scene takes place as the family sit in the deep shadows of their room, not knowing what to do. They are swimming in the disarray of thoughts that are jumping around in their minds like fleas. Gregor's moving about in the sanctuary of his small room activates them as a family as never before. They debate what to do . . . he must eat or drink and they decide to bring him some milk, implying that Gregor, who liked milk before the change, is still endowed with the same sensibilities. Milk. A sign of comfort and dependence. Mother love and yet infantilism. It used to be his favourite drink. Did Kafka's mother put milk on the table? To fatten the almost anorexic Franz? Drink your milk as a symbol for mother's milk and mother love. But now the milk tastes revolting, as does Mother's crawling, smothering, heavy love. So Gregor revolts against milk as he can't against the mother. Milk is repulsive and he spits it out. He has gone beyond the age of milk, he is now a fully grown man/insect. He has left childhood and been catapulted not into a strong, virile male but somehow, as if the genes made a wrong turn in the womb, into a malformed monster. He has severed all ties and it may have been necessary to do it this way. He is now a shiny, strong, repulsive insect. He must be fed scraps, dustbin litter, stale bread, rotting and stinking vegetables, old cheese. But for now they take him the milk, passing the saucer from one person to the other, perfectly miming the dish between the fingers and thumb, and thus we see each one abnegating the odious responsibility of going into Gregor's room.

Eventually it falls to Greta to do it, but the family will accompany her for protection. They slowly walk to the door, with the music building up the apprehension. Father mimes opening the door by stretching out his arm, which becomes the door itself as he appears to open it, and Greta swiftly deposits the saucer on the floor of Gregor's room. They listen outside but hear nothing and we see both Gregor's reaction inside his room and the exterior. Gregor stares at the dish and knows they are outside listening. The family decide to leave him in peace and thus spare Gregor any humiliation he might have in drinking in front of them. They walk slowly back to their stools and as they do so Gregor is seen spitting out the loathsome milk; by the time he has made his speech about the rejection of milk they have sat, and as the lights come up on them, they are discovered slowly and solemnly eating their mournful and joyless breakfast. Now, however, instead of the exuberant, lively, opening breakfast scene, their healthy clockwork ritual, it is slow, painful and nearly tasteless as all their thoughts are on *one place only*. Mother, who can bear the tension no longer, finally has to bring it out into the open and asks her daughter, 'Greta . . . did he . . . drink it?' The next stage is to examine the room and Greta is appointed to go. We focus on the inside of the room with its nightmare lighting effect as she opens the door and then shuts it, rushing back in terror. 'He's under the bed,' she squeals.

Amon, as Gregor, has devised a series of positions based on the original choreography but adapted to suit him so that each time the family expose him by opening the 'door' he is in another shocking or surprising stance which throws them off balance. He is now upside down with his head on the floor and his feet stretched open on the cross-bar. He is becoming more and more insect-like and very unnerving. Greta reports that he hasn't drunk the milk, but it was spilt, so obviously he tried it. The family decide to unite their efforts, to collect some old bits and pieces and see by 'what he leaves, what he likes best' . . . this is one of my fave bits since it is here that we can make a ceremony of the play, an interval of pleasure, a piece of almost Japanese theatre. As they gather the bits and pieces, moulding them and snatching them out of the air, they are able to create them with their hands and we see and almost feel them.

The musicians now add a highly percussive note and the three take on an aspect almost of dance. The piece has in this case become ritualized. They beam with the pleasure of their achievement, but during all this time they have not left their stools except to stretch, gather, shape, stand, so that all actions are clear and defined and they announce them anyway: 'Some nuts, raisins, here's a stale loaf, the remains of last night's stew,' etc., etc., . . . It works very well and takes us away from the tragedy for a few welcome moments of humour. Also it's highly symbolic, since it demonstrates that life can be rekindled when it serves some cause.

Yesterday after rehearsal went to Shinjuku, a vast shopping centre, a wide avenue lined with trees, shops, cafés and outside ice-cream parlours. Suddenly I notice the whey-faced, podgy Westerners whom I have hardly seen before. Of course they are shopping. There is an American base here, so I imagine many of the fat-arses I see are the possessors of some military male on the base. How strange that these gigantic Yankee posteriors could almost become a racial characteristic if programmed long enough into genetic memory. They wear these disgusting appendages with no sense of shame or guilt, used to their own grossness. What a significant symbol of American sleaze fast-food culture.

We slide around the stores and enter a kind of market area where I find a cheap fashion shop that reproduces high styles based on famous designs but for a tenth of the price.

Tuesday 20 October
Go to the theatre where we are to open, to see the Philip Glass opera *Einstein on the Beach*, directed by mod theatre guru Robert Wilson. These two reigning champs of the American avant garde have been taking their epic round the world, setting paths ablaze with works of theatre that many can only dream about. One can be influenced by the Wilson/Glass theatre without ever seeing it. So hopelessly are we, the public, like those sea anemones with a thousand sucking feelers that snatch at anything that passes by without ever seeing what is the object of its desire. I recall Amnon Meskin telling me about *Einstein on the Beach* in Israel in 1978! And like an exotic galactic asteroid it has returned and been spotted over Japan. I have never seen it before, but my own production of *Salomé* could have been influenced by it, not directly but through Amnon, an Israeli director who from the angst-ridden hysteria of Israeli theatre views with gnawing envy the cool, minimalist look of New York. The repetitive, subtly changing rhythms of Glass match the repetitive, changing movements of

Wilson. The programme has photos of two girls in jeans, white shirts and braces – very New York, a tad fringey since the cast don't have to be much more than willing appendages, and there is a touch of Hopper and cafés called The Leaf and Bean. They are singing numbers – 'one, two, three, four' – and you watch and think of New York with a bite of nostalgia . . . cafés in Greenwich Village, Lower Broadway, giant lofts. Thin, bony women with dance companies like Viola Farber . . . Giant steel-framed warehouses that darken the sky and are scarred with the metal laceworks of fire escapes. Taut, sharp mornings on Delancey Street, just off the Bowery, where everyone comes to work clutching small brown bags in which are endless coffees and doughnuts. So all this slowly unfolds while I watch it. A huge two-dimensional train is shunting in from the wings. It is a beautiful cut-out of a steam train.

A girl dancer now treads a path up and down stage, repeating this movement as if there were some secret significance to it, making me struggle with my shadowy knowledge of relativity. Is this significant? And if so, of what? At the moment she looks faintly ridiculous and also reminds me of New York, phoney, helpless against the power of New York culture. A man stands on a metal watch-tower and sometimes throws paper planes. This is Meyerhold via Walt Disney. The engine driver appears now with his pipe . . . image of Yankee sweetness (Rockwell). However it is a haunting image and you can't forget it. It is seared somehow in your mind as if your head had been held by a metal brace, like Malcolm McDowell's in *A Clockwork Orange*. You retain the image as if it has been tattooed on to your frontal lobes. But that is all. Underneath it feels like a two-dimensional image, a man appears to write theories on a blackboard, gestures are arbitrary, having no real way of guiding themselves since they are arrived at vacantly like a mathematical equation that is all wrong but looks pretty. Nothing penetrates deeper into your unconscious, making you alert, moved or concerned. The lighting is well conceived and 'clever', self-conscious, but the whole thing seems like a search for something that has evaded the director. The music holds the pastiche together.

The next scene is the trial . . . the reporters play with their pencils and make serpentine patterns in the air. Two stenographers make waving motions with their hands as they pass over the keys, people choreographically adjust their skirts after too much sitting and the whole detritus of human behaviour is recorded with much care. We see

New York when a group all take the familiar icon, the polystyrene cup, out of their little brown bags and it's all so cute. A voice proceeds to tell us about small-town feminism in Kalamazoo. People wear those mikes around their faces that stupidly remind me of the teeth braces you wear as kids but which are part of the trite, fetishist accessories of dozy pop stars like Madonna. Robert Wilson looks like an efficient bureaucrat who has the ability to drain the humanity out of humans and when they are dead rearrange them into a semblance of life. After two hours we leave and have a pasta.

It's a warm Tuesday in the Seiyo Hotel and the lounge has a calm, warm, wintry feeling, glowing primrose lampshades, flowers, quiet-footed waitresses in black and white calmly delivering oblations. All the businessmen here look as if they fiddle their tax. I have eaten a club sandwich for tea which will obliterate my gnawing hunger for supper and in this halfway-house mood am utterly useless for anything. Today I completed the lodger scene with Yuji, who is very funny; we give him the greatest entrance on earth and he simply adores it. It's lovely to see an actor relish his biz. He has a long, Bach-like entrance as he slowly walks in like a prince rescuing some damsel, but here the family look on as if he were the saviour of all their dreams. The Japanese actresses said sweetly that they wished to work with me for ever, so I can't have been doing so badly, and since this is a very different opinion from the one Mari expressed in rather colourful terms about her last British director (apparently the worst experience of her working life), I feel justifiably smug.

Israel, 1978

I believe the long entrance for the lodger started in Israel when I was invited by Amnon Meskin to direct Met *in Haifa just after we had had a huge hit with it in the Nimrod Theatre, Sydney. After two days in London I flew to Israel to begin it all over again.*

This was my first time in Israel for nine years. In 1969 I went there as an assistant to Wolf Mankowitz on a film of mindless banality called Bloomfield. *It is about an Israeli footballer (really), played of course by the arch goy Richard Harris, who saves a cute little boy who was cast in London notwithstanding the fact that Israeli children are the most beautiful on earth. So with this piece of garbage we shunted into the Dan Hotel, Tel Aviv, and I proceeded to have the worst time of my life. I had just finished directing my first* Met, *at the Round House, and Wolf suggested that I come along as an assistant. After my theatrical triumph I felt I had sunk into the cesspit. In 1969 London was in full shagging swing, skirts were up to the knickers and everyone was a trifle daft. Everything was sex, nudity on stage was almost compulsory and Roman Polanski was everywhere. My aversion to all that leaping about came from my belief in theatre disciplines suvh as gymnastics, mime and ensemble techniques, while all around me was this sleazy circus, culminating to my mind in Peter Brook losing his balance and giving in to the mood of the time by unveiling a huge golden prick on stage at the end of his* Oedipus – *a production that anyway owed much to the uncredited Living Theatre techniques devised by Julian Beck, also to Joe Chaikin. In fact, the techniques that were current at the time in the American underground theatre.*

I had gone to the Kameri Theatre in Tel Aviv and desperately tried to interest them in Met, *but to no avail, even when I presented the best reviews and comments about the great Jewish writer, Kafka. But nine years later an actress from the Haifa Theatre Company saw it during a revival in London and her enthusiasm persuaded the sluggish administration to perform it. (Admins are usually sluggish, moribund and dull since they live with the theatre, planning every day, and it must be very hard to summon up any enthusiasm for anything.)*

Amnon met me at the airport on a hot night in Tel Aviv and we drove to Haifa. He asked an odd question: 'Did you bring the tape of the music?' In most theatres in the West, music and sound effects are canned and that is thought quite normal, but I have seldom used canned music and deem the live interaction with performance necessary and organic, vital to the growth of a living performance. Here, already corrupted by the lazy attitudes of the West, Amnon looked for a tape. I said no, we had to have a musician on stage playing along with the actors. He was visibly taken aback, as he hadn't auditioned or even budgeted for a musician, but the next day calls were made and one was found. A hard, bony, sinewy percussionist came in and we started. He was a friend of Asher Sarfaty, who was playing Gregor. His name was Zohar Levy and he was a man who loved women and was, I think, spoilt by an ever-adoring mother. An intense Iraqi Jew, he poured his passion into the drum and we hit it off and created some very exciting sounds. Asher had trained at the Webber-Douglas School of Drama, where I taught mime in 1967 and where he had luckily been when the balloon went up in Israel. So the gentle, supine, wistful, blossom-filled squares of South Kensington with gentle summer skies and codswallop plays, and the freedom to sit on the outside wall between classes and have a half-pint on the corner replaced the battle for Jerusalem.

Asher was a goodish pupil with much passion and desire and always looked as if he had just got out of bed. When I started my own group with Kafka's In a Penal Colony *I asked Asher to be in it as the non-speaking guard and even in that he was very good. He got bored after a few months, but after what was for him a fruitless time in England and when the war was won in Israel and everything had returned to normal, he went back to Tel Aviv and recreated* Penal Colony *there. Now ten years later I was in Haifa and Asher was a young bull. Seeing him after the lightness of Australia seemed a little strange and at first we met awkwardly, having been so close at one time. Now he was a full-grown man with a wife and small child and I had moved far away from the world we shared ten years earlier. Asher had trained for the part of Gregor, running daily along the beach in Tel Aviv and working on his arms so as to be able to be free on the scaffold. No longer the winsome, dreamy and passionate youth, but a toughened man; still aggressive and seemingly devoted to me and the kind of work that we do. Asher was a joker, unpredictable, unafraid, immensely strong and with a touch of the gangster about him. He liked the fact that in many bars in Tel Aviv he was known as a star and got free beer. He was a brilliant Gregor and worked very hard at it; he combined power and a deep tenderness which his Jewishness brought out. The whole production was much more emotional than the Australian one I had just done, which was to be expected, although the Aussies were awfully good too; it's just that the Jew playing such a subject seemed already to be in touch with that psychic infirmity, that sense of not belonging. I loved directing it, even if it was the second time in three months, since it all seemed fresh in that wonderfully expressive language.*

I liked the special Viennese coffee house I found to sit and write in, round the corner from the Haifa theatre. Then each Friday, since we would finish early for the Sabbath, both Zohar and Asher would say, 'Coming to Tel Aviv?' since Haifa was rather a quiet town with little to do except trawl around the beautiful food market and admire the giant avocados and big orange persimmons.

I was given a flat high in the Haifa hills and I recall going down the road to my little grocery store and thinking how Shelley, my wife, would find all this so charming and admire my fast-growing Hebrew vocabulary. But alas, and for whatever reason, she never did come. In those days we were both busy chasing round the earth and she was always in dance class or choreographing for her group. I was beginning to feel a bit isolated there, even with the occasional trip into Tel Aviv or Jerusalem and the warm, ever-giving company of Asher and Zohar. I was locked away in my flat. Every morning I worked on a play I was writing about Jesus, based on a book I discovered in Israel called The Trial of Jesus; *I sat at my desk with the Bible open in front of me, and this remarkable book, by Chaim Cohn, posits the theory that the Jews have never defended themselves of the charge of deicide, and in which the author, an ex-Chief Justice of Israel, sets out to disprove what he feels were contradictions and inventions in the New Testament.*

At other times I formed the rather anarchic habit of throwing mouldy tomatoes on to the roof of the opposite building and observing with interest how many weeks they would lie there before rotting into the concrete. Sometimes the roof was a veritable salad.

I would either walk down the hill to the theatre or a taxi would pick me up and we'd wind our way down into the town. We had an old rehearsal room and worked hard and eventually the memory of Oz faded and we created a show with even more power than before.

Devorah, who played the mother, had the most difficult time, since the scourge of the Western world, naturalism, had infested all societies and they had found a rather sweet, middle-aged actress to play the rôle – she was the 'right age', but of course it was hard for her to cope with the timing and movement, which needed considerable energy. Eventually, after a few kvetches and tears, she broke through and became very good. Naturalism is such a restrictive art form!

Some days we rehearsed in Tel Aviv since some of the cast lived there. After rehearsal Asher would go to the beach where, as on all Israeli beaches, there was an exercise bar. It was a chin-up bar and since Asher had been training hard for the climbing he had been working out on the beach. Quite nice, when I come to think of it, to live in Tel Aviv just off Dizengoff Street and be able to wander down to the beach for a glorious swim and some exercise and then sit in a coffee shop after listening to the latest news of the border clashes.

Anyway, we looked at the exercise bar, which was not very high, just a few inches from my fingertips, and Asher, seeing my hesitation since I was loth to slip, called out playfully, 'Come on, have some courage and jump' . . . I was wounded that my ex-pupil, for whom I had been such an emblem of bravery, should use that word to inspire me to action. I felt very guilty. Asher had become a raging tearaway, fighting and arguing at the drop of a hat from his manic testosterone balls. So I felt suddenly awkward with him, as if he had stuck a pin into this delicate balloon called the male ego. But how could he have done that, since I never cast myself in the rôle of strutting macho and never wished to? I had too much female, which ironically was my strength. I loved movement, pantomime, gesture, music and had more affinity with Marceau than Marciano and yet somehow there were left in my genes flecks of that old Russian herring pickler, my grandfather. Perhaps I felt I was betraying those remaining genes somewhere, hence the guilt. If I had more of them perhaps I would have less of the inventor, the director, the teacher, the sculptor of movement. Asher was still an actor, strutting his wares. But I liked him and he gave a blindingly passionate performance, funny, vulgar, sensitive, sweet and comic. He was a huge public and critical success and has to have been one of the best Gregors.

Zohar was acclaimed for his extraordinary, expressive music played on a multitude of instruments, but since then he seems to have been haunting a backwater. The actor playing the father was a delicate performer but I think lacked some of the fire needed for the part; however, he had a certain style and lyrical quality. The mother, Devorah, started to enjoy it, and the lodger was the strangest-looking man I have ever seen, a man of such gentleness that I was very drawn to him. His name was Shmuel Wolff, and his face looked like an exaggerated El Greco, a model for Don Quixote. When I came back to Israel to direct Agamemnon I used to go to his home for Friday night supper, Sabbath supper, i.e. chicken soup and all the trimmings made by his attractive wife. Sometimes during rehearsals of Agamemnon, when the chorus were getting into full swing, I would mime drinking soup, since he made me feel I could visit him any time. He was a friend of Asher and had been introduced to me as a candidate for the lodger. This weird, thin, gangly man, broken-toothed, large-domed skull covered with thin wisps of hair, made his entrance one of the most spectacular ever devised. It was slow, stately, transcendental, as if an angel was coming to save the family. He walked on slowly in his white suit, an emissary from the island of hope. So from that moment all my future productions would have that slow, stately, beautiful entrance accompanied by passionate, Bach-like chords.

I loved living in Israel and writing my play there in the morning. In the evening I would sometimes eat at the house of Amnon Meskin, one of the directors of the Haifa Theatre, who was a great, ebullient, warm soul with much love of life and a huge voice he had inherited from his famous actor *father. Since then I have directed* The Trial *in Tel Aviv and even* Kvetch *with Asher, but it all slips away compared with the memories of* Metamorphosis *and* Agamemnon. *It is the actors who make it memorable and Asher, in spite of difficulties at times, always made it so since he is always so alive and vital. For* Agamemnon *I had a wonderful actress from New York called Joanna Peled to play Clytemnestra. They didn't like her way of speaking Hebrew but to me she looked and sounded incredible and she became a friend too. Zohar did the music and Shmuel Wolff was memorable in the chorus. It was an incredible and indelible experience in which I pulled out every inventive stop I could. That was in 1979 and it smells like yesterday. I miss Israel deeply – the weekends in Jerusalem and the unique and atmospheric American Colony Hotel and walking round the old city.*

Wednesday 21 October, Seiyo Hotel

Felt wretchedly isolated last night until I received an unexpected call from a chap whose brother knew me in London. He picks me up in his Ferrari, which has great power and drive but feels a tad tinny, and we zoom through the Tokyo metropolis with me feeling as if I were in the movie *Blade Runner*. He turns out to be a most fascinating chap, an investor working for insurance companies who trawls the Far East looking for clients in whom to invest hundreds of millions of dollars. He says things like, 'New Zealand is my client,' and he means it. So we embark on a debate about the emerging capitalist economies of Asia and the Third World. I venture the opinion that China's strength came from embracing Communism so that it didn't go the way of religion-dominated pseudo-democracies like India and other moth-eaten, corrupt and ridiculous régimes where people climb on rubbish heaps or in the economic-miracle societies like the Philippines. These fast-growing economies seem to have a lot of shanty towns but fast-growing for what and for whom? So we ramble on and scramble among the pages of literature on which he, for a businessman, is surprisingly well-informed, and he passes the comment that he was so impressed by my performance in *Salomé* that he is surprised not to see me play more Shakespeare! Yes, I think, it is a shame. Here I am doing *Met* for the tenth time and I could barely drag myself to rehearsal yesterday. Each time I do it I make it different and alter, add, refine, but basically I am working with the same story and the power to exact a live experience from it, for me, lessens. I did my all in New York

with Mischa on the twentieth anniversary of *Met* and no doubt I will
do it at some revival in 2009 when I am seventy-two! God forbid. If I
could let a rehearsal director take it for a while it would lessen the
pain. Sometimes I can get very involved and stand up there and
enthuse with the actors in the joy of the creation, and at other times I
stare at the fixed minutes of the clock.

Dream. Nightclub. Home.
Dreamed all night . . . mustn't indulge my craving for sake so much
before bed. Am in an East End night club and my ex-boxer friend
Jimmy is there, but there is a younger blond tyke who bullies me and
makes me feel deeply uncomfortable. A bit of a tearaway, handsome,
loutish, who has formed some connection with me. I hasten to be rid
of him. Then I am at home and I have an adorable young woman in my
bed. However – and this dream seems familiar – my mother is outside
the bedroom door and then my sister and then my father come in. I
wish almost to hide my companion. Then I see my auntie Betty and
there is an attitude of criticism in the air, a feeling that what I have
done is somehow not quite right and rather unwholesome; yet I crave
my lady in the bed with a deep longing.

Wake up in the morning knowing I can't take two more weeks,
impossible, and not even at my slim, five-hour stretch. I shall be well
finished this week and so perhaps I can take a few days off or just work
at full pitch so I will not notice. Mishima, the writer who committed
hara kiri, did it opposite the restaurant where we ate yesterday in the
grounds of the Ministry of Defence. He was protesting against a
demilitarized Japan. Apparently he did not do it quite right, although
in the circumstances I think he did it very bravely and I don't think I
could have done it better. According to my new English friend he
should have disembowelled himself and let the stomach fall out,
holding it with one hand while cutting his throat with the other. Simple
enough, and he should have stuck to it, but instead was decapitated by
a friend. I like the still, early mornings in the Seiyo Hotel before the
world gets up and I can calmly unwind my life with Kafka . . .

London, 1969
*It was boiling at the Round House in July 1969, and nobody in those days
had even heard of air-conditioning.*

My first production of Met *was a triumphant critical success, but I had no invitation, no expression of curiosity, or desire from any quarter to go anywhere. No matter, I had done this myself and what it did for my ego was colossal. I knew that if I was to get anywhere in this land I would have to do it myself and rely on no one, since I had discovered that everyone was out for himself. And nothing deterred 'administrators' more than if you walked with an unfamiliar beat.*

After the splendidly bizarre and talented Maggie Jordan joined us in a 1972 revival we toured Newcastle, Edinburgh, Cardiff, a ghastly little theatre in a back street which was the most depressing time of my younger life. We had the choice of sleeping in a cheap bed and breakfast or a caravan; we thought the latter would be romantic and so we did, all of us in two caravans, but they smelled damp and plastic. I was now relegated to playing the lodger, since I had given up my rôle to Terry McGinity in order to create my company and tempt actors with the plum rôles; I let myself be carried along in the wake of others' endeavours. After the succès d'estime we should have been picked up and transported to Broadway. However, we soldiered on until we reached the Hampstead Theatre Club. By the time we revived Met *again, Jeannie James had rejoined the company as Mother, but sadly, after Maggie, she looked a little too conventional and her movement no longer worked with the company's, which was now expanding and experimenting, adding new colours and becoming, if anything, more Kafkaesque.*

By the time we got to Brighton we decided to give ourselves something more to do to be creative. That is where the short pieces of Kafka were invented and we did these strange and lovely aphorisms as a curtain-raiser. I did a short story called 'The Bucket-Rider' and so we had a forty-five-minute series of sketches before the main piece, but eventually dropped them. I went on to develop other works with the group and we did Macbeth, Miss Julie, The Fall of the House of Usher, *and then my own original play* East, *but since* Met *was so popular we kept reviving it.*

Wednesday 21 October, p.m.

After I explode at the poor Yankee businessman who was talking in a loud voice in my sanctuary, the breakfast room, I find myself on the mobile doing the very same thing at breakfast! My accountants have rung from LA in answer to my query about money. I am now a businessman sitting in the lovely Seiyo Hotel talking money to LA! I can qualify for the gross award. Anyway, I am tired of being an 'artist'.

Yesterday's rehearsal goes well after a terrible night. I stagger in, determined to throw myself into it as the only means of escape. The father is back from judging a beauty contest and tells me confidentially that the lines aren't sticking in his head; I am not surprised if his social life doesn't give him the time to learn them. However, he looks concerned and I know that he has been having a rough ride so far in trying to keep up with the women.

I concentrate hard this morning to get rid of a multitude of obsessions and find that I can burn them out. The actors have a break and come off the stage pouring with sweat from their vigour. We start with what I call the domestic scenes just for a warm-up, the scenes of family disputes that don't concern Gregor. We work on ways of using the three stools and seeing them not merely as places to put our bums but as platforms for our forms, mini-stages, daises where we place moving sculpture. In this production we reduce naturalistic moves such as walking across to another person to talk and then walking back. Here they are synthesized into gestures of leaning in or leaning back, contracting the body to reflect whatever it is feeling and thinking, and using a multitude of other gestures to synthesize movement and give the audience no doubt about what is transpiring. Legs open, straight out or crossed resting, but not just sitting. Imagining a back to the chair. It is a stool in front of a fireplace where you sit low and ponder; it is a throne, a high chair, a samurai chair, a child's small chair, a chair at dinner, at breakfast and all at the same place. The cast also reflect each other and react to each other.

So today we attempt to find a way into one of the domestic scenes which seem a touch too wordy and floppy. It is the scene in which they discuss Gregor's predicament and the mother and father differ widely about the contribution Gregor made to the household, with the father naturally trying to diminish it. The mother winds up her husband by implying that Gregor kept them and the house from suffering any hardship only through a great deal of self-sacrifice, etc. Mr Samsa is made to feel guilty since Gregor has indeed scurried about like a veritable insect to fulfil the daily needs. It is a longish scene and we use a method of expressing the words as if they were blows to the body – as each accusation hits home it causes a withdrawal as it draws blood. It makes for an exciting and interesting image but even there it has its limits.

As they argue I want the scene to disintegrate somehow, as if their plight were tearing the fabric of the family apart. The words hurt, accuse and fly, but it is the noise that torments Gregor as well as the content of the row – the raised voices, the shouting accusations. So at the end of the scene I suggest that the actors mouth further imprecations against each other while the drum rolls backwards and forwards, suggesting the fury of their encounter as the two shake fists, gesticulate, bare teeth, rise from their stools and sit again. The drum 'speaks' for them and it creates a weird scenario as if you were watching a fight at a distance and could only imagine the terrible things the combatants were saying to each other. The imagination is always more vivid when it has to fill in gaps. The concealed is always more alluring than the revealed. Greta covers her ears, Mr Samsa climaxes the scene by raising his fists as if to strike her, perhaps for the first time in his life, and Mrs Samsa rises to meet him and doesn't cower, nails ready to make tracks in his face. They stand like two primordial beasts quivering with rage, face to face, neither of them able to strike first.

Eventually the obscene futility of the gesture robs Mr Samsa of further will and he breaks off suddenly, as does Mrs Samsa; and both go to their separate rooms. It will be, I hope, a more telling scene; I am pleased to have found yet another way.

Certain scenes stay in my mind and this one in the LA production is one of them. Priscilla Smith, a highly respected New York actress, was trying out the swaying back and forth as the insults and accusations flew. This didn't seem to work or they couldn't get the rhythm and so we opted instead for Mr Samsa to leave the stool in disgust and go up and downstage with Mrs Samsa following; as he reached the acme of his movement she would catch up and then he would come downstage. They resembled two large caged cats as she pursued her quarry who could only escape by walking up and down until the climax. It worked and looked and sounded perfect, but Priscilla didn't care for it. What made it work when I tried it was the fury you could get into your body as you cornered at the end of the walk, all the time accusing, haranguing. Eventually we did it sitting and it was fine, but never as exciting as when they moved.

After the break we do the dinner scene, which looks like pure Kabuki. They take the potato, look at it, drool, eyes crossed in anticipation of pleasure, mouth wide open to pop it in. They sense that other hungry eyes are on them; put the potato down and slide it along the table to the next actor, who repeats the ritual. This is one of the times when mime not only does the scene for you, it positively creates something that would be utterly impossible in a 'real' situation. I make the discovery that realism can't work to show the inner person, but only the outer, since the gestures of realism are too small, having to accommodate the mirror.

Thursday 22 October
Went to my first movie in Japan and saw Ridley Scott's *Columbus*. Like anywhere else in the world, the repulsive habit of eating in cinemas has taken hold in Japan and the enjoyment of the film is far more elusive as crunching and sucking noises ensure you are pulled out of the total involvement that cinema is supposed to guarantee. *Columbus* is an impressive-looking film, but lacks metaphor and vibrancy. All these battles become wearying after a time and a dash of intellect rather than bold facts wouldn't go amiss. Eventually the maker of commercials reveals his lack of intellectual muscle when tackling a subject that badly needs some intelligent evaluation. For this one must refer back to Herzog's *Aguirre, Wrath of God*, with no battles but a brilliant screenplay underpinned by the late and lamented Klaus Kinski. The conflict between church and temporal power was again rehashed with the usual dull clichés and waspish vicars of God whom one must appease as they sit in magisterial gloom and dispense wisdom with the effort it takes to fart when sitting; small wimpish squeaks coming out of their stinking, ordered and regimented brains – and has it changed today?, I ask myself.

In the morning go heavy-hearted to work since I lack two actors, but am able to develop the lodger scene. It is looking very good since Yuji is a natural mime and is enjoyable to watch. The father again is less effective and has to be almost dragged along, like one of those wounded figures who fall by the wayside on some Andean expedition. However, in some scenes he makes progress. I watch the clock like a hawk and again relish the domestic scenes. The scene I so liked of the father and mother having a raging argument to a drum while silently mouthing their words looks bad and 'clever, clever' today; strangely, what I thought was so brilliant before, I now cut. It could be because I am lacking one of the musicians who played the drum. Fairly obvious answer. The danger of having the production up and running with over two weeks to go is that out of my boredom or false sense of guilt for the actors (quite unnecessary, as it happens) I feel obliged to

embellish, just to give them a feeling that we are still 'discovering' . . .
I even resurrect another image of a beetle created from the multiple
image of the family and one I last used a decade ago. We play with it
for a bit and I fancy it might work, and it surely would have done with
some application, but my confidence isn't in it and it is quickly
relegated back to the cupboard. I must not be a hypocrite, sitting and
sitting and getting bored. I must be honest . . . say I have had enough
. . . let them rehearse and go on holiday for a couple of days.

Back at 5 p.m.
Back in the large rehearsal room, the full set is up and it all looks very
good and Amon, the bug, now fits into it very well . . . I enter late and
a mite sluggish but decide, since cameras are recording for NK TV, to
rehearse from the beginning with the Chief Clerk. He's still far too
stiff and inflexible . . . I feel myself getting annoyed and say ironically
that we have a year to do this scene. I seem to shock him into loosening
up; the scene improves and it looks better than ever before. For the
most part, the Japanese are beautiful to direct, so easy and flowing.
The language acts as barrier to the superficial discussion so beloved of
the more cerebral director. Here the actors watch with great care,
picking up on body gestures swiftly and I find I am allowing more of
my own imagination to flow into it than ever before. The music is like
a sound track from a Kurosawa film and the scenes when the family
are united in effort, such as feeding Gregor, are quite beautiful – the
actors almost dance to the music and their bodies take on the rhythms
of a ritual.

The Japanese actresses are very beautiful to look at with their lovely
raven-black hair and even features. They bounce off each other's
gestures like jazz musicians spinning off each other's notes and the
scene of the 'last potato' is never funnier. When they go into their
reverie of how Gregor used to toil for them, we have a flashback of
Christmases past and see Gregor slowly slide out of his cage and enter
the world of the family. Before, we had always staged this scene with
the family rising and becoming a little trio upstage, but now they
remain seated and stare into their thoughts as Gregor moves close to
them. They don't see him except in their dreams. They toast him as if
he were with them. It is a very moving scene and Amon is totally in the
spirit of it. Greta plays the violin since Gregor is paying for her
lessons; we hear the sweet, pungent sounds of Puccini, then suddenly

the taped music goes dead. She is playing as if in a nightmare when no sounds come out. Gregor accuses the father of taking the money intended for Greta's lessons. The son now leaps on the father and attempts to throttle him, the age-old struggle between father and son, as one tries to usurp the rôle of the other. Mr Samsa merely rises from the stool with Gregor like a child round his neck, moves backwards to the cage and throws him into his room. He then returns triumphantly to his stool as if he had merely flicked off a fly. By one of those wonderful chances of nature, whereby you are given an unexpected gift, this scene is lit in an extraordinary way. There is a front light used on stage to create giant shadows on a cyclorama that stretches across the stage and is very powerful for certain scenes. When I use this front light to illuminate the size of the threatening father, I notice that just before he sits and his legs are stretched apart one can see between those two colossal enlarged trunks the rounded back of Gregor on his ramp, looking exactly like the silhouette of a bug. As Father sits he appears either to crush the bug or even to absorb it by some monstrous act of ingestion. So the perspective from the front is of a vast, black, threatening shadow crushing poor Gregor flat, as symbolically we are invited to believe Mr Samsa, alias Herman Kafka (Franz's father), did to his son. Thus *Metamorphosis* was born. It is one of the most powerful images of the play and is given me as a bonus. Gifts have a certain beautiful purity about them.

Thursday 22 October, 11 p.m.

As I lie tired in mind and body with a sense of utter hopelessness and meaninglessness, I reflect upon the work I have achieved in the past year. I tend to chew upon something nourishing when I need consoling – like an animal chewing its cud, I chew my memories. So far this year I have remounted *Salomé* and *The Trial* for a tour of Australia and Japan which lasted three months and which received the highest plaudits whenever it played. Did my London première of *Acapulco* at the King's Head, which was a popular hit and we didn't even transfer the thing. Then flew back again to Japan to mount this year's fourth major production. In the writing stakes, devised a modern version of *Agamemnon*, which I entitled *Revenge* and set in the modern-day East End. Last year performed and directed *The Trial* at the National. Directed *Coriolanus* in Munich while writing a book about it, and directed and acted in my own play *Kvetch* in the West

End and the Edinburgh Festival. I like to think also that each has been a triumph and not just another production to shove on stage to fill a gap, so I now feel I need a reward beyond 'it is its own reward'. Some emotional psychic upheaval.

My mother once played the piano and one of the things she liked to repeat was the story of her father taking her piano away when she was fifteen so that she would go to work. That she was a prodigy and might easily have been a great concert pianist I have no doubt. Even in middle age, when I was a toddler, whenever there was a piano she would get on it and play the memories of her childhood; her fingers darted over the keys at the speed of light, making the odd mistake but I could imagine her playing like a fiend when she was not more than nine or ten, since she used to play for the school in assembly. Her brother, my uncle Alf, a boxer, bought her the piano from his winnings in the ring; I can envisage the excitement in the house in Batty Street in the East End when the piano arrived in the year 1910 or thereabouts. But what made him get her the piano? Perhaps there was one at school that she tinkled on or at a neighbour's and she expressed a wish for one of her own. My mother, Polly, was the youngest of eleven children, no doubt pampered by her older siblings – would her father really have got rid of the piano when it might have caused offence to Uncle Alf and when she probably entertained everyone at home? But according to her, Grandad encouraged her to work in an office and the temptation to go to the West End, to meet boys and flirt, must have been overwhelming; perhaps she just grew fed up with the constant learning. However, my mother's story is about the oppressive Mr Samsa figure who robbed the frail and helpless child of her legacy in life. And of course we all believed every word Ma said. There was no reason not to.

So if the germ of inspiration trickles down the generation from mother to son, then it would explain why one day I woke up with an almost overwhelming need to learn the secrets of those black and white keys. Keys to the soul and the spirit. Keys to a universe beyond dreams. Keys to magic. My thirst to play was insurmountable and I would rush to the piano whenever I found myself near one in a neighbour's house, or a club, school, wherever, and I would try to unscramble the mystery of those keys as if I could somehow pluck out the secret, but I could only jangle the spirits down there – they need graceful stroking before they will reveal their combination. Sometimes a relative or friend who knew a few secrets would teach me a tiny fragment of Grieg's piano concerto, which I could play on all the black keys, and I would cling to these few notes, playing them endlessly until I could find new ones. This went on for years, a pleading, crying, begging, yearning until the obsession wore itself out. Mother's musical talent erupted in me like some dormant volcano when I was in my thirties and I took lessons and even reached a moderate rendition of Mozart's Etude in C, but then the last fling of my unconscious faded out and I was at last left in peace; I had transferred my desires to performing as an actor and could play other notes. I recall that each morning in Düsseldorf when I was directing *The Trial* I could not work with a peaceful mind until I had an hour on the piano to quell the whining child that would be appeased.

My own father reminded me of Mr Samsa. He was an archetype of the East End dad, brought up in times of struggle and viewing achievement as the very first rung on the ladder towards climbing out of economic despondency. When my mother's genes reappeared in me, she would not have seen my yearning for a piano as an echo of her own struggle but as a childish whim, like a whim for a bike or other toy or a dog; by then she had no doubt been brutalized by my father, who appeared to have not the slightest taste for music or for books – his only recreation was playing cards and seeing how much money he could lose at the greyhounds. So when I came to play Mr Samsa I created a brutish but somehow innocent father, bullying by reflex, shouting because it was the only way he knew to assert his power, sentimental at heart; I played him in as comical a way as I could.

Many male actors cannot really parody themselves if they are of the right age to play a rôle. They take Mr Samsa seriously and do not step outside the character to see how to highlight those extraordinary aspects of the Prussian, stiff-necked behaviour that is ingrained in the male stereotype. As performers and comics we are able easily to parody the foibles of women, especially in panto, and we are besieged by drag actors. But who parodies the excesses of men in all their lurid obscenities and petty habits? Women are funny merely for having breasts, fat arses, silly voices, bizarre dresses, weird hats; the audience chortles as the panto dame comes on to pour scorn on the 'inferior' sex. So I chose to pour some scorn on the male and at the same time make *him* an object of humour and ridicule. Male satirists are awfully good at doing women, but less good at doing themselves, except for people like Chaplin or a great actor like Olivier who could create a bizarre gallery of male freaks.

Again, choosing to find a mirror image in the story since it is easy to do so, I too had a sister, although not in the sense of the secret intimacy that Gregor had with Greta. My own mother was like Mrs Samsa, emotionally warm, concerned and devoted to her one son. Perhaps through the difficulties and shortages of the war certain things had to be denied, but my mother's music came out instead in my obsessive desire to dance, which I seemed to spend my youth doing, starting with waltzes, foxtrots, moving on to sambas, cha cha cha, the jive, the twist; whatever new set of rules came along I would absorb them. When I staged *Met* for the first time it was full of rhythms; the rhythms of daily activities ritualized into rhythmic beats. This stylization took it away from the musicless world of naturalism and yet paradoxically heightened the simplicity of what you take for granted and gave it an almost spiritual overtone, if that word if not too precious an epithet to adorn it with. I could say that we then stood back and observed them as if watching some animalistic pattern that wove their lives together.

The second time I staged *Met* I added live music to highlight and underline gesture, mood, atmosphere, and so eventually my frustrated musical desires did come out; I was able to put my rhythm and my need for music into the theatre, even to the extent of eventually attempting to write verse.

Watching Mari and Atsuko work is like watching and hearing musicians – particularly Mari, since she is like a piece of moving sculpture. That this form and control in an actress hardly exists in Britain doesn't really surprise me, since there seems to be an obsession with academia and interpreting the texts like fusty scholars. Although Shakespeare had a very good head for music, one wouldn't know it watching those interpretations where the director believes that, like Dickens's Gradgrind, the text is in five beats and thus it should go . . . thump, thump, thump, thump (pause). Shakespeare's text is curiously uneven in its versifying since it goes from verse to prose and even the verse sometimes dribbles over its ten iambic beats. The verse is more like a river whose banks are uneven but which keeps a continual flow and so there can be no rule, unlike the verse of Molière or Racine with its determined and fixed beats.

Last night after rehearsal went with Yoko to an expensive sushi where they seem to charge what they like and a meal can cost a small fortune, and then drifted around the Ginza district looking into the print shops at those exquisite Japanese drawings which seem to capture an extraordinary atmosphere with a few simple strokes and an extraordinary use of primal colours.

Tomorrow Off!

Run-through very poor. It runs 1.45, a tad long, and I am rather disappointed in the work but take a lot of notes and go back and work through them – it improves radically. It is good to get the first run out of my system . . . the first time you endure it and the actors can't remember what follows, but then at the re-run and stops for notes we improve all three domestic scenes. When I arrive today it is so sunny that we sit outside and bathe ourselves in it before facing the windowless gloom of the basement. Masumi, the father, gives me (like teacher) a big juicy apple.

London and Sydney, 1976

I actually revived Met *for just a few performances at the National Theatre in 1976 while at the same time I had* East *on at the Regent Poly, now sadly closed with additional help from Brian Rix who wouldn't let us extend on a slighty reduced rent. Market values = one dead theatre. I had two shows of my own running simultaneously in London and on my birthday the two casts assembled at the Zanzibar for a birthday drink. As usual, it wasn't a great party but I was very proud. While we were doing* East, *Michael Halifax, then the general manager of the National, was trying to fill the gaps in the Cottesloe's season, since the new régime hadn't yet got all its own shows under way. The Cottesloe's early mandate and the reason for the third theatre was to give other theatres round the country a London house so that it would be truly a 'national' theatre. Sadly this wasn't to be. The third theatre became less and less available to other performers and theatres and was swallowed by the monolith. However, at this time we were plugging a few holes for Michael Halifax and glad to do so, since we, or I, mistakenly as it happened, felt that we were a kind of associate, ready not only to step in when the gaps were yawning but in a planned way as a possible yearly season. We did three or four performances of* Met *and then Michael came with his giant diary and said we could do another show here and there, and so we did* The Fall of the House of Usher. *We had actually started there with eight performances of* East. *Eventually the National had their seasons sewn up, our endeavours to put* shows on at painfully short notice and to achieve full houses went apparently unappreciated and we were not invited back for fourteen years! However, there were other theatres and that's where we went. You might ask if we or I misbehaved or created some disturbance, but the truth is we were an exemplary company which played to packed houses and to cheers, and I was even celebrated in a Sunday Times profile for having had three plays on at the National at the same time! But perhaps that was a little unacceptable . . . you never can tell.

Following a successful season at the New London, Drury Lane, which we rented for a short time and which might have been our repertory theatre, we went to Australia with our production of East. We all fell instantly in love with Australia, not knowing what to expect but never dreaming it had such beautiful cities, wide open avenues, brilliant mornings, adventure, open skies, new tastes, frangipani on the morning pavement. East went well and I decided to do Met over there and so I redirected it at a small theatre in Sydney. I was now almost a native, since after four months of East I was to stay another two. My cast was very good and George Shevtsov, an Australian of Hungarian descent, played Dad very well. I enjoyed the rehearsals and the feeling of camaraderie, and found an excellent Gregor and friend in Ralph Cotterill, an ex-RSC actor who fled ship when Brook's circumnavigating Dream reached Australian shores. After long tours in foreign countries actors often drop off and stay. When West Side Story came to London it seemed as if half the cast stayed on and flourished there. It was amazing to me that with all their energy and ambition they didn't find it irksome and dull in London, but they found work as choreographers; dancer Gary Cockrell started the whole modern dance-class craze in London and virtually brought American dance to the city before the Graham school came there. So a few actors had stopped off there and decided they liked it so much they wanted to stay, and why not?

Sydney would have been a glorious idyll for Ulysses. A city of sirens and lush papayas and a warm, glorious, surfy sea at Bondi to swim in every morning. What bliss! Ralph was a Peter Pan, a pixie with an ever-ready smile. He introduced me to his yoga master in Bondi, a disciple of the yoga master Iyenga, and after these torture sessions I felt as if I was becoming a rehabilitated human being. Ralph and his mates all lived together in a kind of commune house in the Sydney suburbs and you were always welcome there – the atmosphere was loving and full of natural, easy freedom. They became, in a way, my gang; we hung out a lot in an elegant café in King's

Cross. I felt for the first time that I had a 'group' and we'd watch the sunsets from the café terrace which were extremely beautiful and I spent my time with my Pentax snapping them up.

I felt the full benefits of my 8 a.m. yoga classes and when I came out seemed to tingle in every pore of my body. I have tried to do some yoga ever since. Ralph worked with extreme zeal on his bug and we would go to the workshops where the set had been built and practise every variation and position. The play opened in Sydney to absolute rave notices and was quickly sold out. I was delighted with one particular review which said words to the effect that one should not be too influenced by the panache and earthiness of East *with its streetwise jargon, since the* Metamorphosis *was an intellect at work! Well, thank God someone noticed.*

We rehearsed in a hot, stuffy rehearsal room and the music was like a delicate tapestry flowing through. It was composed and played by Nick Lyons, who also became an ally. It seemed easy to make friends in Oz in their classless and likeable society. Warren Mitchell also became a friend and we teamed up from time to time, but I was suffering exhaustion of one kind or another and started to feel isolated and missed home.

The next year they decided to transfer the play to Melbourne and so I made my way back to Oz and redirected the cast. I stayed at the beautiful Windsor Hotel, where Xavier Hollander of the 'Happy Hooker' fame was also staying, although I never availed myself of the services she so kindly offered. I again gave classes, which is an enjoyable way of communicating with the theatrical world in any city. The show was a sell-out in Melbourne, and I went back to Sydney and reluctantly parted company with Oz to return to London. I like the strangeness of Australia, its heavy, warm, autumn rains, hot, damp afternoons, Bondi in the summer and half deserted in the autumn, Tamarama Bay, outdoor cafés, great breakfasts.

I returned in 1982 for a twelve-week tour of The Fall of the House of Usher *which was prefaced by my one-man version of* The Tell-Tale Heart . . . *I recall this trip taken ten years ago with immense detail since I believe I was under not a little strain at the time, but it was resolved and the show received mighty plaudits.*

The next time was 1992 with a six-week tour of Salomé, *and I can hardly recall it, so blandly did it pass by, but I still stirred up the cappuccino froth of Bondi, still had breakfasts out there and walked to Tamarama beach. Perth had improved beyond recognition and it was one of my happier times in Oz, just as it had been one of my worst times ten years ago. Ralph Cotterill came to see us at the Seymour Centre and still*

84

looked elfin-like, even though he must be approaching sixty. How those who have journeyed along the same path have unknowingly entwined around each other some human bond of loving friendship. Curiously enough I formed strong and everlasting relationships with all the Gregors I have worked with excepting two; one of those was Roman Polanski, who, sadly, seemed to have little to say to me after rehearsals and found it a little difficult to take direction, but that is probably because he had not really been on the stage for so many years and was extremely cautious. Brad Davis from LA I liked very much; alas now dead, and I mourn him, for he was a good soul and an ally and I shall never forget his powerful energy. He was shaped like an Apollo and was a sensitive and gentle person.

Friday 23 October

Thank God! A day off! I think I have had enough and one can have enough. Worked Sunday, Monday, Tues., Wed., Thurs. and so it is normal, for God's sake. I watched the run-through with a growing sense of unease as the events shuddered into each other and so much of that painfully evolved and complex movement was forgotten. As I watched the Japanese Dad flounder, I came to the conclusion that René Auberjonois may have struggled with the rôle in New York, although I thought him an excellently inventive actor, because I was unconsciously trying to lay *my* Dad on him and René is not me. My suit did not fit him and it had to be recut to fit René. When I created Dad I felt he was all fathers, just as Maggie Jordan's Mother was all mothers. It wasn't a question of great acting but of putting at the actor's disposal all the arts of movement and mimicry to create a polyglot, multiform attitude of man. When I raised my voice as Mr Samsa it was from anger built on a plinth of comedy and self-mockery. When René shouted he was terrifyingly real, but he eventually lost his voice and missed some performances. This was my fault, since I should have been able to direct such a clever actor as René along the Brechtian lines of stepping outside one's reality and presenting a social group, but sometimes it is difficult to direct actors 'out' of naturalistic impersonation without appearing to 'demonstrate' and have the actor copy which is not satisfying either.

Now, and for what reason I cannot judge, out of all the productions I have done, there has never been a Father who stood out or who really took off except, as I said earlier, the first one, George Little. He played it seriously and yet 'comically' and was excellent. With George the rôle didn't grow into the deformed and exaggerated character it was to be, and some might say all the better for that, and yet it had style and verve; the underrated George Little, a good jobbing actor, is still very much a part of the theatrical world today.

Curiously, all the women who played mother and daughter were brilliant. Mothers: Jeannie James 1. Maggie Jordan 2. Priscilla Smith (LA) 3. Laura Esterman (NY) 4. Linda Marlowe 5. etc., etc., etc., and now our skilled Japanese lady Mari, who perhaps is the most unusual of them all and a beauty to boot! All the women, from London to LA, from Toyko to Israel, wiped their husbands off the stage with consummate ease (hopefully yours truly excepted). Therefore I am probably saying that women are better when they have a chance of emotionally releasing the torrents of energy in their acting, while men are stiffer and less able to emote. But when men do, of course, it is quite breathtaking for being that much rarer. The young men who played Gregor fared better, Terry McGinity I think being one of the best of them; not as athletic or as biting as Tim Roth's harsh, bitter portrayal in 1986, but in sheer, huge emotion he overwhelmed the part and was both a tough and a moving bug. One cannot forget his strangely beautiful and resonant voice, his flaming red hair and his satanic looks as he was escorted by his mother to his milk (a flashback long since discarded). It was a strange, deeply compelling performance which had me revise my own vocal limitations since Terry's voice had such dignity and range.

Some fathers have been such disasters that they have almost sabotaged the production and I am thinking now of both Paris and Düsseldorf, where I had no hand in casting and where supreme miscasting meant that the actors were chosen for being merely older actors rather than performers. Exactly the same mistake happened in George Lavelli's celebrated production of *Greek*, in which the dad, who is meant to be a powerhouse of working-class emotion, was played and cast according to a satiric description of Eddy's when rudely addressing Dad: 'His face hung there like a soggy, worn-out testicle.' Well, the actor they found to do it didn't look too well on the night and I feared the demands of the part might even bring about his demise. The problems of naturalism. If the character's old, get an old actor. Hence, the power and energy of a quarter of the play was totally out of joint and when Eddy had a fight with the café owner/Dad it was such a foregone conclusion who would win that it made a mockery of the scene. Luc-Antoine Diquero, the boy playing Eddy, was, however, brillant – I have never seen anything like it in my life and I am sure that no actor in England could come even close to his range. He was trained at the École Jacques Lecoq and worked in straight theatre for years, but with his own idiosyncratic flavour. He had actually taken the rôle over from Richard Fontana, who was one of the most celebrated actors in France, was on loan from the Comédie Française and whose performance was not a whit less than his successor and who in fact created the ideas for the rôle. Sadly this young, vibrant actor fell victim to AIDS and it was one of the greatest losses to the French theatre. That they had another boy who could so easily take over and recreate the incredible physical pyrotechnics says something about the health of the French theatre.

You need language to train your vocal and physical muscles and give them the opportunity to gallop. There are not many opportunities in the British theatre to do that since everyone is so busy being lifelike and realistic that their armature and network of muscular reflexes are sadly sagging and when a young actor comes into my production full of the verve and passion to extend himself fully, I actually worry that once he is out there all that potential will gradually fade. Here in Japan the father, as I perhaps by now overstated, is miscast, although gradually working himself into the rôle. If I had a choice I would have chosen Zero Mostel in New York, Toshiro Mifune in Tokyo and perhaps Robert Hirsch in Paris. Olivier of course would have been perfect.

While women seem to be more naturally given to venting their emotional ducts than men, they generally have to do this in secondary rôles, hence perhaps the great success of homosexual actors who are able to merge both male and female characteristics and so have it both ways! They are in charge of the great rôles, since men are generally thrust centre stage by the male bastion of playwrights and have the sensibilities of their female side to give them that extra vibrancy . . . It must be galling to women to have to take for granted the endless parade of male woes, pride, confessions written by male writers as if the female were some kind of appendage to man. Usually directed by a male, the females trot along to see how Hamlet makes out with these stupidly underwritten women around who all seem to be in the throes of PMT while the men carefully enunciate the philosophy that will be quoted for all time. The Ancient Greeks knew how to write for women and what formidable heroines they created, so perhaps in those days playwrights were more interested in the power of the female archetypes than in puerile male ambition. The female was the balance to the male and while Agamemnon was busy killing for honour in Troy, Clytemnestra was ruling a kingdom and would eventually kill her husband in revenge for his having slain their daughter for a sacrifice. It seemed to be a balance between two forces rather than a single force supported by an adoring appendage. I feel that in *Metamorphosis* male and female are in perfect balance and that Kafka drew clear pictures of the whole family, even if they are seen through the eyes of Gregor.

Last night went out with Kashiko, the wife of my film producer of *Decadence*, Lance Reynolds, who acted as a kind of charming host to me in Japan. We decided to visit a disco which I believe was on the borders of hell. More lightning explosions than the Gulf War, a mindless, gormless entertainment for the masses. Deafening, heartless, soulless, tasteless. Mass culture at the lowest possible level where the last shreds of human dignity are hanging on by threads. The total lobotomized anthropoid. Somewhere behind the ape, behind the first stirrings of awareness. Smoke rises, lights spin round at random, without direction or aim, without harmony or pattern, just light like the mindless rock and roll it accompanies, the next best thing to being smashed over the head with a beer bottle. Culture turns in on itself and dies. I saw death of civilization in that disco and yet I like both dancing and music. I enjoy the sensation of moving, learning new dance techniques. So in this ear-piercing disco a seething mass of flaying arms impersonated underwater antennae, moving this way and that with no purpose or will, but driven by the force of the music which dominated everything like a noxious gas. Conversation impossible, only shouting. Like an airport, they had a VIP lounge where you paid extra but were insulated from the blast and made to feel that out of the throng of human flotsam you were one degree better. From our vantage point we saw the sea of arms waving in the air and the bodies jigged up and down in an aimless pneumatic motion that everyone duplicated; no one was different. It was a mass that abnegated any ideas of individualism, as if that might be too heavy a burden to bear, and would rather melt into the waxy mob oozing backwards and forwards to Yankee pop. The crowd was strangely composed of many Japanese gentlemen in suits and ties and the roving lights, each like a leering eye, shed its beams first on one part of the deadly mass and then another, like the sun pouring through rents in the clouds to expose hell. There is no doubt that flat-liner has arrived. The joyless Orwellian jog, a masturbatory group gesture . . . this was less art than a monkey picking its arse and maybe this is what mass culture has become, monkeys picking their arses or Madonna flashing hers. Is the Apocalypse coming?

Saturday 24 October, 10 a.m.

Seiyo Hotel breakfast. Impossible to write . . . every time you poise your pen someone comes with a basket of croissants, refills your tea, takes a plate, removes a fork. While sitting in the lounge I hear the Yankee-speak, it's always the same sound, little variations in tone or nuance. How come the homogeneity – television? American TV announcers have this bland, slightly heavy, nasal tone suggesting that everything is OK. Little colour and playing on two and a half notes. After hearing the wild arpeggios of Japanese for weeks, the American voice seems flat. The Japanese is swift, rises suddenly and then ends in a dying fall; it's musical and mercurial, and when I see these overweight sacks of flesh among the slim of Tokyo, these ill-dressed sloppy tourists among the beautiful crisp, black-suited office girls of Ginza, I get quite depressed.

So waiting for Yoko I hear and see these tourists or business couples complimenting the manager of the Seiyo Hotel. The male has his hair in the style of Crosby, Stills and Nash, or is it Art Garfunkel? The front of the hair has disappeared and the rest of it is piled around the crown like a kind of halo. He is celebrating the hotel in oleaginous LA tones. 'My wife,' he mouths proudly, 'is one of the leading immigration lawyers in the United States; she writes the books that other lawyers read.' The man, from what I overhear, has something to do with writing about hotels in Asia and advertising them in the USA. His talk is thick with how important so and so was and we had dinner with the head of toilets and industry. He becomes very funny and I only wish I could remember the garbage that sustains his life. Then another person sits down and he actually repeats the whole boring spiel, like a tacky salesman.

Yoko arrives and we go to the Kabuki to see Taramisubu, a celebrated Kabuki actor, in a short play about a woman who takes on the spirit of Japan. The actor seems to be able to express peony blossoms falling slowly, leaves waving in the wind, being tossed this way and that, and he uses just a fan or sometimes a pair of fans to express the leaves falling, waving ready to drop, and then the rain. A lion comes to rest and shelter in the perfume of the peonies and while sitting there he is disturbed by a pair of butterflies dancing around him and tries to catch them. His performance is very elegant and very beautiful; his delicate hands are as fluid as silk handkerchieves; they float through the air and co-ordinate superbly with the rest of his body. This is by way of being a prologue and now he leaves the stage and we hear some music being played for several minutes while he changes. Next we see an extraordinary change of perspective, as if from the lion's point of view, since the actor, rather than telling the story symbolically with fans, becomes the lion itself and enters strikingly and powerfully with a huge lion wig. Two children become butterflies. Taramisubu's dancing/mime of the lions is quite exquisite and the lion's wig seems a concentration of both wig and tail; he whips it around his head and it magically takes on the animalistic features of the lion. I love the wide open spaces of the Kabuki Theatre with its panoramic stage, the audience munching beautifully arranged little boxes of sushi that are sold in the foyer of the many eating areas. We are invited to go backstage to greet the master. He is a very unassuming young man who is already surrounded by his admirers, in the centre of whom he holds court while sitting on the floor with his legs modestly to one side like a woman. We are served green tea and make light chat about how long it took to rehearse, and, since the piece was first created over a hundred years ago, how one can find a movement language to recall the piece. One element which impressed me while I was watching what I called the prologue was his dexterity in handling the fans. At one point he threw both of them in the air; they somersaulted and he caught both of them almost as if they had magically flown into his hands like carrier pigeons. I was acutely nervous that each time he did it he might drop one, but of course he never did. Nevertheless, as I watched I wondered to myself what on earth he would do if he did drop one, since I felt it would kill his act and throw a shadow over his mastery. The whole audience was on edge and he was not concentrating on a single fan but had to divide his attention to catch two! I was calculating the odds of failure and I thought, would it be worth it to get it right fifty times but on the fifty-first to drop it and lose all face by having to bend down to pick it up?

Caught out in front of the public, like throwing a foil in *Hamlet* and dropping it . . . oooowwww! How embarrassing. To avoid the one in fifty I might be tempted to aim for a fail-safe device like, for example, miming an object.

So in this mood I ask him if he has ever dropped a fan and to my great surprise he says, 'Yes' and adds, 'three times!' In a way that is a great lesson to me. I say, 'What do you do when that happens?'

He answers simply, 'I pick it up, or if it drops a little way away my assistant, who is crouched there the whole time, retrieves it for me.'

The audience, he says, are shocked, some gasp, and they worry for him! So after this relevation I begin to revise my attitude. Surely it is worth doing something risky, even if you drop a fan once a week, just for the satisfaction of doing something breathtaking six times a week. The Japanese ego is far more at ease with its position with the audience than the Western one that fears humiliation. So in one night I learn something.

Taramisubu is a charming and attractive young man and seems used to the ritual of receiving visitors in his dressing room. He says that Baryshnikov came earlier in the year and spoke of his experience in New York with me directing him in *Metamorphosis*. I can see Mischa in there smiling and sitting cross-legged, drinking green tea.

Go home after a mandatory sushi and watch the great American movie *A Tree Grows in Brooklyn*, directed by Elia Kazan. I soon weary, though, of its wholesomeness and stock characters but it is certainly a worthy movie.

Sunday 25 October: A Strange Weekend
Finished a very good run on Saturday afternoon and am pleased, moved and proud since my producer Susumi is in and says it is far better than expected. I always like it when somebody comes to see the show after weeks of work and I am able to show all the magic tricks, new ideas, shapes, inventions. As soon as a friend comes I almost burst with excitement and live the whole show all over again, trying to sense every vibration of the visitor. Then Susumi and his assistant, Yuki, whisk me off on a promised trip to the country since Susumi believes in looking after his 'artists' and visitors, unlike some producers I know. We cab to the station and take an immaculate train to the countryside, not far from Mount Fuji. The train is spotless and the station full of life: shops, cafés, bars, newspaper shops, all lively, active; succulent

box lunches are sold for the journey and there are magazines in the rack as in planes. We dive into our bright, sparkling train and half sleep until we come to the small village where Susumi has booked a Japanese inn called a ryokan. We alight, jump into a waiting cab and alight again at the ryokan, where we take off our shoes, register and walk past a stream that runs through the inn to our rooms. The two large rooms are pure Kurosawa; bamboo screen, straw-filled mats, sliding doors – a demi-paradise of tranquillity, form, space and light. My room is uncluttered by any heavy furniture, and simplicity, order and harmony reign supreme. There is just a table in the centre and a long balcony outside where a rapidly flowing river gurgles past over stones. It is like a haiku poem. 'If the mind is not at rest then water over stone washes away bad thoughts.'

In such places of supreme calm and idyllic beauty the warts tend to sprout out of your brain, unable to survive in such a clear environment, and I watch Susumi take out his Nikon camera with flash and record all these memorable things. Suddenly I am transported to a place that must be what we call hell, since my great protuberant Nikon with its phallic lens has no flash (which I could so easily have bought) and so my camera is impotent when the light starts to fail. Susumi's camera is lighter, simpler, complex in its guts, but practical and smooth and he is able to take those night shots while my camera lies like a dumb guest at a dinner party . . . A lady knocks gently on the door and, kneeling, opens the sliding door and enters with the most extraordinary banquet I have ever seen, sushi, pickled vegetables, every variety of shelled creature that crawls the surface of the deep; soup, salad, noodles, sweets and so it goes on and on. The sake is hot and we keep pouring it. Just before this we wrapped ourselves in kimonos and trod down the long corridors in our slippers and had an immersion in the hot mineral baths. We lay there peacefully and looked out of the window which we could see from our reclining position; the trees and distant hills made a perfect backdrop. We washed before entering the bath, since you bathe to relax and enjoy the soothing effect of the mineral baths and to chat to your friends, a far cry from the stinking steam baths in London with their permanent odour of sweat and institution. Now we are chatting in our room with Yuki and he is taking pictures of the sumptuous spread and then of both of us on the balcony. I just manage an exterior shot before the light fails.

We get through the dinner and bathe again, which is a relief, and then return to the room to sleep, which soon washes over me as the water makes soft swishes and plops, trickles and babblings; I sink into a sweet, healing sleep and wake refreshed. We bathe, of course, and then breakfast comes, looking like a reprise from the night before. We walk round the small town taking pictures and this time my Nikon comes to life and I can function once more. We visit some Buddhist temples and museums and in one temple I am taken by a story that is illustrated in a picture with a translation by the side. It is the story of a shogun who was killed by rivals but whose wife-to-be chose to be killed first in his place. Apparently he was having a mask of his face made of wood and each time the maker attempted the mask it kept turning into the features of a dead man. The mask maker kept trying until he could achieve a life-enhancing look rather than the deathly expression. After several attempts the shogun saw it and was satisfied. His future wife saw that the enemies were invading and decided to wear his mask to save her man. However, although his life was slightly prolonged, he eventually succumbed and joined her in the afterworld. This later became a famous Kabuki play.

Next go to a park where there is an English model village. In the village centre stands a double-decker red bus, a number 38! How many times have I taken that bus from Islington to the West End? I grab the pole that you grip hold of as you run for the bus and pull yourself on. I have grabbed that pole many thousands of times! We then take the train back and I am somehow glad to be back in the Seiyo Hotel.

Monday 26 October

The thing starts again, the relentless week. Breakfast and a couple of hours to snatch some private life before going into the factory. Might slide off the route today. Don't feel so good. Went to bed early last night and watched a few minutes of *The Empire Strikes Back* on the TV . . . I was in a way looking forward to some escapist sci-fi, but, advanced as the techniques were, the human element was banal and painful to endure. My desire was for spectacle, other worlds and knights carrying the code of chivalry, since it was based on the Kurosawa masterpiece *The Hidden Fortress*, but while I was enchanted by that film and overawed by the sheer majesty of Toshiro Mifune's powerful portrayal of a general for the shogun escorting a princess into safe territory, I had the utmost difficulty in even beginning to believe in Luke Skywalker. I turned the TV off and went back to reading what really interested me. The book on mass culture by John Carey, *Intellectuals and the Masses*, which my friend Ray Cooper gave me, is I think just brilliant and allows me to see how art from the masses has always been as suspect as the masses themselves. It set off many chords in my being and I was able to see how little good work from the working classes is ever allowed to surface in the cultural establishment.

Tuesday 27 October

Yesterday we ran the play once more and rehearsed trivial bits to give the impression that it is still in need of flecks of paint, but it is finished and now constant rehearsal invites spoliation, you must not take something over the edge. Like cooking, there is a time when you must take it off the heat or it will harden and grow tasteless. Now, like a young wine, it must be decanted in the fresh air of the audience. To cook those bits that are still a little soft, like the two men who are not up to the women, will mean over-cooking the women and even now I see in the mother a tendency to exaggerate.

The sun is shining down brightly over the Seiyo Hotel and my little assistant Meg picks me up as usual, looking like a squirrel or chipmunk with her scrubbed, privileged Japanese face. Yoko continues to delight me with her impressions and quicksilver mind; her inquisitive spirit involves her in continuous adventures. Yoko is certainly my friend to rely on in Japan. Now I must be able to withdraw, to sit there and watch and let them make it their own. The task of the director will soon be over and they will learn to fly themselves and need me less and less. I quite like this part too, when they hardly need you except as a barometer, to let them know if they were up that night or down. The time will come soon when I am just another friend in the dressing room signalling for a word, a few seconds to pass a note. They will start very gradually adding bits of their own business and changing bits of mine that don't feel quite right; they will get legitimate laughs based on the social observation that the gestures underline, but they will push and exaggerate to gain more laughs and the social comment will be blunted and replaced by human eccentricity. However, there will be enough left of the play to make its impact.

So now I am time-wasting. A whole week must go to the dogs in eventless eating and pointless rehearsal. Go somewhere or do something. Call a friend over. Go away somewhere. Arrange something. Do intensive Japanese course. Check maps. I wish to go now. Work over.

Tuesday 27 October p.m.

It is sunny and warm today and the rehearsal-room staff have thoughtfully put some tables outside on the forecourt so we decide to have our 'warm-up' sitting outside in the sun. Suddenly it is all very amiable and the lodger speaks of the time when he busked in the streets of Paris at the Pompidou Centre and made 200 francs in twenty minutes; I see again, in his energetic telling of the proud story, his infectious animation as the lodger. Masumi speaks of a time when he visited Santa Monica, California, to see a Japanese friend who married Henry Miller but eventually divorced him – she now runs a bar in downtown Tokyo. Masumi says that he played ping-pong with Miller when he'd a table set up in his living room. Mari speaks of a beautiful *Threepenny Opera* she saw at the Burgtheater in Vienna and how much she loves Kurt Weill. So we idle away forty minutes and then begin a run which was never so clear or thought out. We change a tad here and there, still cleaning up the final picture, and Meguma brings me my carrot and apple juice which she makes each day at home. When Meguma smiles her eyes disappear completely, which is quite enchanting, and her cheeks bunch up at the same time and make her look like a squirrel, and of course she also speaks most beautiful English.

I admire the Japanese more and more, their easy, well-mannered self assurance, their naked pleasure in simple things, their camaraderie at the bar of a sushi house, noisy chatting, drinking sake, never intrusive, affable and liable to talk to you with the few words of English they know. Not one solitary image of violence, snobbishness, yobbism, and not even the vaguest appearance of London on a Saturday night as the pubs disgorge their teeming lager louts. No louts here. Here it is difficult only to drink since there is food everywhere, but the drunken ones are out in force after the office closes, happily sozzled, leaning on each other as they make their way into the immaculate tube station.

I like the cafés under the bridges where the property is cheap and you sit with the throngs outside, wreathed in blue smoke from the teriyaki and yakitori, drinking hot sake or beer, eating chicken on skewers. I suppose they are the greasy-spoon caffs, except they are also works of art. Each café looks interesting and usually each one's name is printed on the cloth that hangs over the sliding door. The kitchen will not only be immaculate, free of fat, grease, burnt onions, it will also be a temple of organization no matter how small or large and it will cater to dozens of different tastes, unlike the ubiquitous sushi houses in the West. Food in every variety imaginable and the fast-food stall in the street with the traffic of Tokyo belching past will still serve up a tasty noodle soup. In Japan these noodle soups are giant troughs, huge bowls brimming with vegetables, noodles and chicken or fish; one will be a whole meal in itself, it will cost three pounds and will fill you to bursting. The city hums with an awesome flow of energy and Ginza Street near me is the size of Oxford Street with the quality of Bond Street. Cafés in every style on earth, from English tea shop to French patisserie, from Italian hi-tech, Nippon style to Japanese, and everywhere the perfect service, care, devotion, neatness, cleanliness, tastiness, calm, sanctuary. And the women are slim, sleek, black-haired and very attractive.

Thursday 29 October

Ran bits and pieces yesterday since the cast wish to check over tiny elements of the play, now feeling confident with the main thrust of their performances, but this causes a rash of irrelevant questions. Not having to deal with the complete run and the demand that it makes to carry the rehearsal straight through for the one and three-quarter hours leads them into nit-picking and stop and start. The music, which was perfect the day before, becomes snagged and bitty and even the musician now asks some utterly irrelevant questions. Then the Chief Clerk starts asking questions like a schoolkid. Oh well, I suppose familiarity has made me too blunt to other people's needs. We continue to forge through, still finding new elements, saturated as the play is with detail and business. The chorus work is knitting together and it is exciting to see this happening. It has such power, a trio compared to one man's puff of ego.

Before rehearsal we again sit outside in the sun – it has now become a habit for us to relax and chat for half an hour before commencing. Yuji, the lodger, has a moon-like face that expresses wonderful degrees of ecstasy in his performance. The sunlight is bright and shines harshly on Mari's make-up which looks streaked and pinky-white, and yet how beautiful she looks onstage. Of course, she is very attractive offstage, but the beauty of the stage is that it projects the real essence of the being at a distance; all surface detail falls away and the core of the person comes through . . . the bone, shape, eyes, lips, outline and colour.

We work on Amon's movements as the beetle, helping him to move less frenetically and more mechanically. (I'm writing at breakfast in the Seiyo Hotel and there is a breakfast business meeting at 7 a.m. with much talk of the Japanese economy. Time-Life is leading the discussion and talking about Japanese launch unless 'the economy is terrible, terrible, terrible'.)

Masumi has an injured back from swinging the women round like a maypole. He is fifty-seven and doing well for his age, but can't quite cope with some of the physical demands. He is not quite as fit as a Berkovian actor has to be, which is not to say that he has to be a Schwarzenegger or a Baryshnikov, but he needs stamina. The years of easy ways have unfortunately not tested him and so two of my best bits have bitten the dust. However, I am sure when he is better they will come back, since Masumi is a very proud man and will not like to think he can't do something. When Gregor leaps on his father's back accusing him of stealing the money it becomes an archetypical image between father and son. Also an image of Jacob wrestling with the angel. The light from the stage floor lights their combined bodies fantastically on the backdrop. The father walks backwards with the struggling thing on his huge, fatherly back and when he gets to Gregor's room tips him off unceremoniously, like a coal dealer delivering coal, and then returns to his seat. The light reveals Gregor through his legs and as he sits he appears to crush him. We have already detailed that bit of biz, but I repeat it since it means so much to me. Now Masumi can't carry Gregor, so we have to devise a way for Gregor to be dragged back instead of carried; the effect may be dampened but I don't wish for an injured actor.

The next effect we have to cancel is when the women pull Mr Samsa off his murderous assault on Gregor. As they pull him off, grabbing him by his throat, they lock their arms round his neck to make him desist. Samsa pulls this way and that like a trapped bull; then he spins round as if to shake them off and as he turns they become airborne like a maypole. Their feet leave the ground, their legs spin round almost at forty-five degrees until he grows tired and gradually the spinning stops and they all crumple. Afterwards they seem to resemble an old trio, or rather an elderly father being slowly escorted to his seat by his dutiful family, since in mime one shape leads to another and this neatly fits into Gregor's speech when he says, 'Could that have been you, Father . . . you used to lie so wearily sunk in your bed when I set off for work in the morning, who could never rise to your feet but only raise a feeble arm, who used to welcome me home at night still in your dressing gown, where did you get such strength . . .?' So all this came from letting a movement grow and find its free associations and was one of the most successful investigations and inventions of the play. Now this most remarkable of discoveries may have to bite the dust, or at least the first part until Masumi recovers, but even without the whirling it still looks good and is powerful in its latter half.

Amon is improving daily and as a dancer he is finding even more permutations for his insect than Baryshnikov, who found quite a few. There are times when he is perfectly insect-like and one sees him with his totally innocent and cherubic face attached to his implacable rigid and multi-limbed body. His pathos is the most touching. Atsuko, the sister, continues to play each run at full pelt. This tiny creature has the energy of a racehorse. Her wiry body seems to be all nerve and battery, and when she screams as she sees Gregor's body through the open bedroom door for the first time her piercing decibel level shatters the room. She also seems to retain the essence of childhood and has to work in Japan in experimental theatre. Her small, unique frame has few opportunities in the commercial world of standardized people. However, this woman is the most dynamic piece of energy I have seen on two legs. Her face has a way of running through all the pains of childhood and her simplicity is very touching since it is the earnest gullibility of a child for whom the simplest pleasures cause ecstasy and the smallest disappointments insurmountable grief.

Yuji continues his foray into the multiple possibilities in the comic view of the greedy lodger and of course his mimetic gifts still enable him to chart some bizarre areas. As the family feed the lodger in an orchestral symphony of eating sounds, he provides the fourth instrument of the quartet as his cheeks flap in and out like a mole. It is one of the funniest things I have ever seen.

Without prejudice, I cannot help but evaluate the conversation taking place at the next table as I write. If you read body language you can also hear speech patterns that act as a kind of subtext to what is being said. The conversation is between a number of Americans and a Japanese businessman. The Japanese is using a very carefully selected combination of words that show him as a man of ethics and culture; he appears well educated, his accent has a literate touch and in English, his second language, he structures good prose. However, his Yankee chums are single-minded and don't filter their words through any cultural sieve to give them colour, so their text is less detailed, down to the bone, no complexity, a touch desperate and stolid. There is always a hint of the implacable in the illiterate since they give themselves fewer options and areas of manoeuvrability. As the cultured Japanese continues to talk in metaphors and even at times sounds professorial, the Yankees punctuate their responses with 'Right! Right!' or 'Sure! Certainly!' The Japanese continues to dominate and hold the stage so that eventually response will almost be impossible, since he will have sapped their confidence by his overwhelming dignity and scholarship. Already they are a bit nervy – they keep clicking their lighters on. The Japanese is still talking and talking. The man is very clever. So clever that all the men, that is the Yankee side, met at 7.15 a.m. and told him to meet them at 8 a.m. So when the Jap arrived at five minutes to eight he viewed the assembled table and said, 'I thought it was eight o' clock.' And they replied, 'You're right, it was eight and you're five minutes early.' Now after the Japanese rodomontade the Yankee speaks. He feels hopelessly outgunned and seems to find it difficult to construct sentences with the same complexity of syntax that had characterized the musical verbal structure of the Japanese.

So happy! After a work-out at the gym, since it has become a real home to me with its pleasant, friendly staff, I sit in my fave café near the gym, Lipton's off the Ginza Dore, and I am perfectly and blissfully at ease. Obviously the endorphins are racing around like delighted sprites tickling my brain and giving me that sense of well-being. I dropped another kilo, so down to eighty kilos from eighty-three when I arrived, but could lose five kilos more. It's a grey, rainy, Tokyo day but exercise renders everything piquant. It's a charming small gym and I have a strange sense of belonging when working out with mostly Japanese men and women. I am now familiar with the girls who run on the treadmill each day with the fixed look as they stare into space and count the minutes on the digital read-out. I watch them bounce up and down like robots and all expression seems to be drained away, all personality – or at least the personality one wears for the world – and what is left is a strange, dozy look, as if slightly drugged, withdrawn. There is nothing else to live for except this moment of running forever on the spot. A little childishness seeps into the faces of the women; they become repulsively fascinating like little dolls being pulled on a string. Sometimes I find myself staring at them in a kind of awe and then once they stop the machine they become normal again. Perhaps I too look like a zombie when on the treadmill. I put it on for just twenty minutes and that does me fine, I try to think of anything to make the time go, even go through speeches. Then, after a few more exercises and some light weights and stretches I leave and feel wonderful afterwards. In the café the pretty young office girls are showing acres of leg, pretending they are unaware as their mini-skirts ride halfway up their thighs.

New York, 1989

I have always been lucky with the lodger ever since we had the original three at the Round House in that hot July of 1969. The three were masked in half masks like harlequins and it suited them very well but Terry McGinity, who took over the beetle, had a go at the single composite lodger and created quite a mad character. Somehow the lodger allows you to tap your unlawful side, the bottled-up, crazy part of you, the childish, anarchic side, and so it has nearly always been very successful. The harlequin aspect of the lodger allows him to react to everything with the brightness of a monkey.

On a visit to Edinburgh we had the Scottish actor-singer Denis Lawson play the lodger; he also joined us in a series of pieces called Knock at the Manor Gate. *After this Matthew Scurfield played an extremely zany lodger with an insane dance at the end. Shmuel Wolff, the delightful lupine character I have already mentioned, played the rôle in Israel and that is where the lodger began his transformation from greedy pig to elegant, white-suited charmer who eventually turns into a pig. We had a good Australian, an effective German, a very good Frenchman, and an excellent actor in Los Angeles called Ebbe Roe-Smith who played both the chief clerk and the lodger in 1982, and thereby hangs a tale.*

When I revived the play seven years later in New York with Mischa I remembered Ebbe's brillant turn in the two parts and cast him to come to New York, but it was a different Ebbe Roe-Smith that I saw. The squalid work situation that exists in LA with few opportunities for good actors to exercise their craft means that one can go to seed while waiting for something to happen, and it it not much different in New York. Ebbe turned up at rehearsal looking much heavier; the old, lithe athleticism, that sparkle he had had, seemed dormant. I had to let him go and he went on to write the biggest-grossing movie script, Falling Down, with Michael Douglas playing the lead!

So then I used Mitch Kreindel, who played so well in Kvetch in LA but while he was fine as the chief clerk he didn't work as the lodger. Meanwhile I had auditioned a Fatty Arbuckle character who was to be general understudy. He was called T. J. Meyers, better known to all of us as just T.J. He had an infectious enthusiasm and while he was happy as Larry to be understudying on Broadway he was more than keen to have a go at the lodger. Our producer, Lars Schmidt, who lived in France for many years and was the widower of Ingrid Bergman, had grave doubts, since T.J.'s experience was mostly as two-dimensional characters in musicals, but he let me try him out. T.J. had difficulty learning the lines, but once they stuck he went – to become the funniest lodger of all. One of his funniest bits of biz was when he first saw the beetle and ran round the stage via the ramp so that it looked as if he was walking at forty-five degrees from the floor. He has extraordinary face muscles which made him at one time look like a pig, and so he fulfilled the lodger to a 'T'.

T.J. was a joy to work with since he was happy and enthusiastic and wanted to please everybody. If Mischa had a backache, sure enough T.J. had a machine that vibrated. He was an entire encyclopedia of aphorisms and was a funny man to boot, with some marvellous impersonations. I have a weakness for actors who can do accents and mime the famous. There is a showbiz myth that those who can 'do' accents are not good actors but somehow have a cheap and trivial facility to capture an echo or trait by impersonation. There are even those who think that stooping to impersonate accents is in some way unredeeming for the great classical actor. I don't remember Gielgud doing an accent in his life, nor Ralph Richardson. Whereas the acting supremo of all time, Olivier, was a master of accents. Brando has a remarkable capacity for dialect and so I think we can shoot down that myth in flames.

The Broadway Metamorphosis, my first Broadway production, was to

try out in Duke's University, North Carolina, where, in the relative safety
of the campus, Mischa could acclimatize himself to the show. It played for
an unprecedented month. I like North Carolina, with its friendly hotel and
small-town American life and simple drugstores where they still make soda
with different-coloured syrups. I sat around those cosy cafés for hours. In
the mornings we were given special passes to use the gym and T.J. would
show me how to play squash. Gary Olsen is another actor with wonderful
manic energy. In the 1986 revival at the Mermaid he played both chief
clerk and lodger and scored a great double act. He had menace, humour
and was a touch bizarre with a hint of football terrace about him. His
lodger was a delight; we played his exit out to the last dregs and he nearly
always got a round. He was good to improvise with and was part of the
new school of actors, along with Tim Roth, who gave the modern version of
the beetle: powerful, alienated, non-romantic or pleading but demanding,
outraged. I like watching rough diamonds become polished, refined, clever
and stylish.

Friday 30 October

It's raining in Tokyo today and we have two days' rest from the show.
The streets are gleaming back the smudged colours from the shop
windows.

The days hurtle by as Pegasus races across the skies of Japan and I
trawl the giant stores of Ginza studying with rapt fascination the most
complex, stunning, gob-smacking, eye-popping variety of food that
human ingenuity can summon. My day off is thus made sweet by
contrast with the now tortuous process of watching something that
should have left the rehearsal room and been put on the stage and so
now feels like an overdue birth. But it is my own pain, the pain of the
success of this story and production that has been demanded and I can
still be moved by it. The production is complex enough to be
interesting and of course the changes it goes through as it journeys
from country to country make it into a nearly new experience. I have
yet to do it in Italian, but maybe I'll give it a miss.

I recall Arthur Miller directing *Death of a Salesman* in Japanese and
I can only imagine what that must be like, to have written a play forty
years ago that you carry round your neck like an albatross, to visit
umpteen productions and to be so PC as to say that the latest one in
the UK was the best interpretation. What! Better than the Lee J.
Cobb, better than the George C. Scott which I saw and which was

magnificent in the round at the Circle in the Square, New York in the seventies? *Death of a Salesman* is a great play, powerful, moving, emotional and an articulate rendering of the heartfelt pain of the common man. A terrible indictment of American values and fast, throw-away society. Willy Loman becomes too old and is consigned to the garbage bin. How awful for the typical rootless, skill-less, craftless, artless salesman who must try and sell something he never had a hand in making. What does Loman sell and does it matter?

Gregor is a salesman. He is diligent and has already returned to the hotel with his morning's orders and sees the other salesman still at breakfast! What does this mean? That the German is a lazy scoundrel and he, the devoted and committed Jew, is zealous? Like Willy Loman, Gregor supports his family and both share a dreadful burden of guilt since both were written by Jewish creators and therefore their heroes must suffer Job-like tests of their worthiness to hold a place in the world. Both Loman and Gregor die from the world's neglect, which pays little attention to their pain. Both are artists, and thanks to Miller Loman is given to rapturous flights of prose. Both empathize keenly with the suffering of humankind, but whereas Miller's empathy is social and he reaches out to the downtrodden and oppressed, Kafka's is introspective and personal. He reaches out to the artist, the outsider and the misfit. Miller's autobiography is searing and very candid; in parts, with references to his love of Marilyn, it becomes terrible and awesome. Kafka's diaries are no less painful, articulate, beautiful. The two men even share similarities of features.

The historic Jew, excluded by law from most arts and crafts, from a thousand possibilities of expressing himself, from landownership to farming, was allowed only a handful of despised professions, which of course included dealing in old clothes, tailoring and usury. So the modern Jew inherits the legacy of the past and Willy Loman and Gregor Samsa return home, exhausted by the system that feeds on them and sucks away at their lives until the flesh falls off Gregor's back and underneath is the stiff, hardening spine that eventually turns into a shell. Loman just wilts and becomes a subspecies, turning his pain into neurotic obsessions, like watering his few plants at night. Poor Willy wishes to make things grow and be responsible for something in which he might see the results of his care and affection. But eventually Willy, like Gregor, decides that he has had enough abuse at the hands of this world, which has wrongly shaped him for a task for which he is not suited.

Arthur Miller now lives in Connecticut on a large spread of land and loves to do the forbidden fruit of carpentry. Something with your 'hands' . . . ah, the Jewish lament to create something real and manual!

It poured down in Tokyo yesterday and I drifted along the black, wet streets past endless elegant shops with kimonos stretched out in the windows like some colourful-skinned beast, sleeves stretched out crucifix-style, and the fall of the exquisite material hanging sharply down with its design of overflowing gardens on the wide border. I stopped by a tea shop and had a lemon tea and watched the umbrellas pass by. As soon as there is the slightest dash of rain all the brollies are out like multi-coloured mushrooms sprouting all over the city.

P.m. Yoko takes me to a restaurant which is small and charming, one of those thousand and one tiny holes in the wall that seat about ten people. I have bought a flash adaptor for my camera and since this caused me some heavy deliberation I am determined to bring it with me and try out my new toy. We have an endless variety of sushi and sake and it seems to cost a small fortune.

On my day off decide to take the train to Kamakura, which is about forty-five minutes away. The relief of getting out of Tokyo is intense and as the city turns into suburb there is a gradual decreasing of tension. I get out the stop before and walk through a charming village until I get to one of the many temples. Without trying to sound like a tourist philistine, when you have seen one Buddhist shrine the others seem remarkably familiar . . .the semi-somnolent figure of Buddha does not vary much . . .the priests wandering around all seem preoccupied in much the same way . . .the wishes for your prayers to be answered are hung up on little wooden plaques everywhere and this pattern is repeated in each temple. There is usually an entrance fee and you wander round looking at a great golden Buddha, or you might see some statuary from the Edo period, but it is the well-kept gardens surrounding the temple which purge your lungs of Tokyo pollutants and your head of the streets and stores of Ginza. Here is peace and tranquillity.

I stop in a small restaurant for some thickly whipped green tea. The food is served in a series of elegant bowls and the little dishes come in a wooden hatbox-like vessel. They are a colourful mixture of everything, perfectly made up, minute portions of every delicacy. You open the box with the anticipation of children and everything looks healthy and clean. You immediately realize why most Japanese are slim – the equivalent in the States would be Burger King and Denny's; no wonder that such great barrels of human fat waddle the high streets of America. Here the food is sophisticated, varied, traditional and brilliantly executed and this is an ordinary, tourist-type café. The great fear among my Japanese colleagues is the contamination of the society by Yankee values. Already the ghastly McDonald's and Dunkin' Donut have dropped their spore in Tokyo. What does Japan export in exchange? Beautiful sushi bars all over America and what do they get back? Rambo, and Madonna's sex book, not to mention the unfortunate instance of contaminated blood producing the first AIDS case in Japan.

Apart from that the whole country is still reeling from the tragedy when a young Japanese boy, a student living in the US, was shot dead on Hallowe'en because in that hysterical gun-crazed society he couldn't understand the word 'freeze'. He was shot dead for his unfortunate ignorance of the country's massive neurosis.

Followed a crowd into a temple compound and felt a furtive pride, like a naughty schoolkid, for sneaking in and saving myself 1500 Yen since I only wanted to linger for twenty minutes and admire the old carpentry. Now I feel I must learn something about it and even take up some chanting. I recall being moved at the sight of people touching the golden figure of the Buddha at Asakasa, and then touching themselves in the places where they felt pain or suffered disease. But then it seems to me that religion is so much self-deception and if you believe strongly enough it may be the code that sets off your own self-healing mechanism. Obviously religion can be the catalyst that releases emotional blockages that may have contributed to the disease in the first place, and so if some emotional catharsis releases blocked emotional energies then you are on the way to cure and you are always somehow reassured by some godlike figure who loves you unconditionally. No matter how ugly, sinned against, unloved, ordinary, plain, disfigured, ill-informed, repellent, stupid, unpopular you may be, if you are a believer there is one out there who, without restraint, pours his love into you. A very powerful stimulant to generate forces in the body that will set forth an explosion of energy and release repressed areas.

Saturday 31 October

The last day of a cruel month. The devastating effect of fixations. If I repress them do they get worse? Of course I know they always come when I am working, getting near to the climax or a first night, and they transfer themselves into little corners as if to relieve me of the huge task ahead, and so all that energy is transferred into minutiae and trivia.

My favourite obsession was destroyed in one blow when I was touring Europe with a production of *Hamlet* in 1980. I had been taking a refresher course in French by working with a book of grammar. As the tour got near I felt I couldn't travel without my French grammar, but it reached a point where as soon as I got on the boat I felt I had to find a quiet corner and get into my studies before I could *allow* myself the pleasure of walking round the boat, chatting to my colleagues, having some fun. I knew that I was in the *grip*. So I calmly walked to the boat rail and threw the offending tome into the swirling waters. I felt beads of sweat pop out of my head in the chilled morning air and I saw my angst float upon the waters and then slowly drown and I was free of it. I could study French if I wished, but would no longer be *compelled*.

But I needed a transference of some kind and so I decided there and then to keep a detailed journal of the play and how I directed from the first line until the last. I wrote the journal until the end of the trip and was halfway through the book the following year when we embarked on another tour. I finally finished the book in 1986. It took me all of five years and it was published by Faber and Faber as *I Am Hamlet*. It achieved some very respectful reviews, since I was totally immersed in the play and wished to convey a round-by-round analysis of my methods. Hence the fruit yielded by transferring some of that energy which fuels obsessions!

Anyway, the point was that I was able to channel the angst into a positive and creative outlet each morning. I loved getting up and being the first at breakfast in some hotel in Germany or Luxembourg and writing it all out.

When Susumi produced his pretty flash Canon camera on our trip I wrestled with the mind wish that I had brought a bloody flash unit with me and in the evening in that beautiful room with the twenty-course dinner I wished I could have photographed it too. Or did I really, and did it matter? Was I not perhaps feeling a little competitive with the young, sharp and attractive Susumi? I viewed my useless Nikon – useless at night, that is – with some disappointment, but how did I transfer that? However, the feeling passed and I recall the same thing in Brazil when I came with my massive phallic Pentax and the suave, elegant first assistant Mark had a small, cute Olympus that he could put in his pocket and whip out when he wished, although the pictures I took were superior and memorable. So all these things were ways of diverting the main angst into small diversions to take my mind off it.

Last night had dinner with Mari and, sadly, hated every minute of it. Feel tired and oppressed. My head is in my coward vein and I am not really there with her. Ghastly slimy things are put in front of me and I actually try to eat one of the shellfish; its texture and taste are just like rubber. I stare at the oyster, wondering at its 'liveness', and decide against it. The fish is enough, but dish after dish keep coming. The tuna sashimi is OK then I have three portions of nigiro, two yellowtail, two tuna and two mackerel, some cooked small fishes and some vegetables and the whole costs 20,000 Yen. A hundred pounds! I paid, though, like *all* Japanese women I have met, Mari wishes to pay for me. Bit of a difference from Western women, most of whom wouldn't dream of putting their hands in their purses.

London 1969

It was a warm April when we rehearsed in the church hall in St Peter Street, Islington, and the hall had a platform or small stage at one end. This served as Gregor's platform from where he could view his family. We had the first reading in my basement flat in Devonia Road. I had not the faintest idea in the world how to begin, but Alison Minto, who was my girlfriend then, helped me evolve a set whereby, since Gregor was on his belly, we would raise him above the family, allowing him to watch them from a distant room. That much we had worked out and then the scaffold had to support the platform, which in turn gradually evolved into a climbing frame for Gregor, which eventually became a piece of sculpture. The steel scaffold started to look like the skeletal frame of a giant insect and all this evolved from the basic need to raise the flattened beetle above the family so he could be seen.

The family, as all families, enjoyed long discussions in the dining room and so we needed something to sit on and decided that what we needed were small metal stools with no back to them so that the family could lean back, twist and turn on them and in fact use them as miniature stages. The family were placed so as to be able to function without masking Gregor from the audience. They sat in a line with space between each stool to swing a cat, and when they wished to communicate they would feel obliged to lean in to the person they were talking to, to demonstrate with their bodies, to use their arms and fingers, to be supple and register all the shades of emotion, since there was nothing to lean on or escape into or hide in. We saw them at breakfast as if the whole front of the stage was a giant long table, but it didn't exist, of course, and they were able to create all the aspects of domestic life from the three stools. What differentiated my theatre from others from the outset was the desire to reproduce the actions of real people artificially. Therefore the actors became artists, not just real bodies feeling things to give life to the subject, but commentators on the way we live, how we eat, what we feel and how we show these things. In the course of this we found it more interesting to dissect our actions and so the family eating accompanied by the metronome broke down the actions and humans suddenly became fascinating. However, we aimed for a heightened reality and so there was still total involvement with the audience. We were not super-marionettes.

To convey the horrors of a giant insect on stage, one has to 'interpret' the story using physical symbols. The man acting the beetle becomes a potent symbol and uses his real human form so expressively that the audience will suspend disbelief, accept the symbol and be moved by it. Not the real thing, for if one took this parochial way of thinking one would then have to have a ghastly piece of stage equipment that always broke down. Of course, such a device would be naturalistic and vulgar, but if actors ploddingly impersonate humans doing real things it is being faithful to the book.

Such rigid thinking also throws a kind of hostility on to any technique used or learned that expands the actor's vocabulary, and so 'naturalistic' directors appreciate actors who have no particular skills since they would not know how to use them. Hence they don't use them or wish to know how. In Metamorphosis the actors' use of the stool as a kind of mini-stage or platform allowed them sometimes to create shapes with their bodies which were quite beautiful, as if they were sculptures on a pedestal; moving mobile sculpture. When Mr Samsa is oppressed by the chief clerk his whole body is able to express his angst as it moves over in a line and one leg juts out to balance it. The three members of the family create this beautiful line, like trees that have been blown in the wind, and the mother resembles a *piece of art nouveau statuary, or a study by Martha Graham. Again, nothing could be more poignant than Atsuko as Greta as she hunches up on her little wilderness of stool, perched there in isolation with her knees pointing in and her toes pointing out – her whole body given to the expression of woe. Being so exposed on these symbolic chairs, each tiny measure, each small gesture is multiplied, since it is exposed outside the confines of naturalistic cosiness.*

Certainly in painting and literature it is possible to put abundant detail on the page and canvas, but on stage the art of the actor is to convey all these details and to use whatever means he or she has to do so. When I saw the theatre in Bali I had a glimmer, although jaded by tourism, of the power of drama that so excited Artauld in the thirties. The theatre was ritualized and served the whole community by acting as a collective, living archive of their myths. A kind of therapeutic dream factory.

Although some movements are afoot, there is little to show of the kind of potential that could be achieved in Britain by increasing the techniques of actors. The two schools of thought are very distant, not that you could say that the naturalistic school had a thought, since it is really predicated on the philosophy of no thought. Just let it happen, be real, and what you cannot convey will be conveyed by stage machinery and props. Great actors can be trained within this system, but here I am really discussing the theatre as a whole and not merely as a vehicle for the star. There are, however, problems which arise even when one is trying to work in the school whereby the actor is the prime moving force, since the indoctrination of naturalism generally means a kind of smothering of effects.

When I was directing a production of The Trial *at the National Theatre, in 1991, the actors 'verbally' described their costumes, since the text of the book was so beautifully detailed. We were then smothered in historically correct suits and dresses which completely softened the impact of their gestures. The designer was a talented man who was used to costumes having to 'tell' the story and telegraph who the characters are, while the poor beast inside flaps his arms around under the weight of expensive garbage. We had to throw out thousands of pounds of clutter before we could see the angles and shapes of the actors' bodies once again, and the movement we had so carefully conceived was revealed in the way I imagine a painting that has been over-painted or 'improved' is stripped bare to show us what it once was. The actors needed only the bare essentials: trousers and waistcoat, a stiff collar told all. So not only does the naturalistic school fail to reveal its actors, it also spreads a kind of fungus over everything it touches. Anyway in 1969 we worked out our first show, which in a way was to be the hallmark of all my future work. The actors were all behind the show and liked experimenting and working with no props.*

Sunday 1 November, 9 a.m.

I saw this man walk slowly from the breakfast room in a rather relaxed and almost deliberate saunter, a rather big chappy, and it turned out to be Colin Davis, who must be conducting here in Tokyo. I need these times in the morning, the sweet peace of isolation, to see nothing or no one but my precious journal and be served breakfast . . . what could be better?

Yesterday ran play. Masumi continues either to overdo it or screw up, but the rest of the company hit just the right note and the play succeeds. Unfortunately the costumes – unusual for the sharp, visual eye of the Japanese – are awful and once again don't resemble the sharp, two-dimensional image of the original design. They are too heavy and dark, but we will improve them. In fact, the best costumes for the show were at the Round House, twenty-three years ago. The women wore long black skirts and white blouses, all black and white and looked perfectly stunning, while the men wore dark waistcoats and white shirts. When we didn't know about costume we seemed to get it right.

So we have the first run-through with costumes, and since this is the last rehearsal here there is a small party afterwards for everybody. It was a very pleasant get-together and I realize how much I have missed having a get-together after work, how soul-satisfying it is. I sense Atsuko's deep disappointment with her costume, which goes against her marvellously tight performance; we need some advice in order to make her look like a little girl. Fortunately this is the last day I have to watch it in this rehearsal room. It's 1 November, I have been here just a month and it has actually flown past. I wish I could watch the jivers in the park with their big Elvis hair-dos and drain-pipe black jeans.

Düsseldorf, 1983

There was a rehearsal room in Düsseldorf from where you could hear the trains rumble past every few minutes. The cast was reasonable except again for the father, who was plainly awful and totally miscast, and the young girl, who was one of these German dolly-birds who pouted and had not the slightest idea how to act or move, but at least she did look like a possible Greta. Unfortunately she thought looking pretty was everything and so the acting was left to Gregor Bernd Jeschek, and the mother, Bigi Fischer, who were both superb. Jeschek had great physical skill and was a most inventive performer; he even looked like a sleek black beetle with his jet-black hair slicked back. It's always the combination that works, sensitive, slim, patient, long-suffering mother and poetic, wounded son, but why do they always give me this kind of Dad? Why is there no equivalent to the female of the species? Why always awkward, badly moving, dull males? However, the hours seemed to creak in Düsseldorf and sometimes I ended up doing just four hours' rehearsal and flying back to London on Friday nights since to be in Düsseldorf on the weekend was like being in purgatory. However, for all that, I had a room in a beautiful inn on the edge of the city and on the Rhine, and I used to watch the boats go past and even take the boat to the Altstadt (old city) and walk from there to work. There was a Japanese garden opposite the hotel and just before breakfast I would struggle with a twenty-minute run, which as usual set me up for the day – I have been doing this sometimes three times a week for the past twelve or more years and always feel the benefits throughout the day. In September the banks of the Rhine are full of spiders and they invade your room, crawling across the ceiling like small, dark silhouettes. At first they scared the hell out of me, since I do suffer somewhat from arachnophobia and kept imagining one of the beasts dropping on me during the night. In the morning they would be vacuumed up by the cleaner, but when I returned in the evening they were there again.

I had an assistant and now it starts flooding back as if memory were covered in a layer of dust and you needed to blow on it to reveal the details of the picture. Perhaps concentrating, meditating on the event is a form of cleaning the canvas. Estella Schmidt, my assistant, was an Austrian who lived in England. She was of extreme-Left persuasion and had been at university with the theatre administrator, Günther Beelitz. She had obviously been close to him at one time, since he always offered her a job as my assistant as she didn't have many opportunities in England. She was basically employed as a dramaturge, which meant she translated my English version, took a percentage of my royalties and created a thick mine of information for the programme, full of quotable nuggets of wisdom from contemporary European hi-tech philosophers expounding on Kafka. Much interpretation was to be found in these epic tomes, and psycho-babble, plus photos of the family of Kafka. For the poster I had the idea, since Bernd was so extremely agile, of photographing him in a dozen different poses and then making up a poster of a hundred pictures, the way we were photographed years ago with a sheet of dozens of positions and you would choose one. His various positions were then used as a recurring theme throughout the poster, like a design motif on a piece of wallpaper. Bernd was a daring and strong performer, the only actor I have worked with who could swing himself out of the cage and on to the ceiling in one ape-like swoop. I tried and tried, but my fingers kept being pulled open by my weight and also my fear.

The production was very successful, but of course with reservations. The first night came and it was well received, so I clambered on the stage in good old European style and then we all piled into the restaurant next door and had to pay for our own first-night celebratory party! I thought this was a rather shabby way of treating a guest director, but obviously word had filtered down since some actors had made whiny complaints to the Intendant, who then decided to punish me. However, when a cultural tour from Japan came seeking German theatre to tour Japan, out of all the shows they saw in Düsseldorf they chose mine. A couple of years later I received a card from Bernd saying how grateful he was for the opportunity to visit Japan, made possible only by this show.

Many companies who take Metamorphosis into their repertoire find that they have a little nugget that provides international currency and can penetrate areas with which they hitherto had difficulty. My Israeli production created a huge stir in Munich and although I was not invited to go since I was only the director and adaptor, the play received standing ovations and the Germans were much moved by the 'great' Israeli theatre. Ironically, when I was directing in Israel, the theatre there was going down the tube with terrible productions with an awful Western bias; Neil Simon was the big hit of Habima, Israel's national theatre, while The Trial was taken off after only a couple of dozen performances. Yet when Habima wanted to show off their great ensemble work and theatrical skill on a world tour to Canada they took The Trial and were, as usual, fêted.

Brussels, 1988

I took a quick trip to Brussels just after Polanski had played a very acceptable beetle in Paris. The Théâtre du Poche (pocket theatre) which, true to its name, was a little theatre in a charming park, decided it too would like to stage the show, but this was too small even for me and I thought I would give the job to the very able assistant who had worked with me on the Paris production. So the arrangement was that since Kirsty Haas had worked with me painstakingly on the Paris production (pain being the operative word) and knew every move, she would plot the moves, supervise the music and I would come for the last week to 'polish'. This would give her a badly needed job and I would still be earning from my employer.

The day came to earn my wages and I flew to Brussels. By the strangest coincidence my next Gregor was there, Mischa Baryshnikov. He was in Brussels to see the Mark Morris dance group.

I duly visited the Théâtre du Poche and was quietly appalled at the cut-down set and the quality of actors. They had tried and meant well, but even if you know the moves it of course still needs a modicum of physical skill to interpret or even reproduce. Unfortunately Kirsty was unable to suggest the spark behind the moves and it was my job to sort it out.

I watched in a kind of dumb horror, secretly relieved that I hadn't asked Mischa to see this awkward, miscast hash. I then suggested some changes and we all had a break and dinner together, which was very pleasant and I think out of relief and nerves the actors drank too much. The next morning at my hotel I received a call from the theatre to inform me that the actor playing the father had been knocked down by a car as he was crossing the park and was in hospital with a broken leg, poor man. (Again, troubles with the father.) I was asked to rehearse with the others until they found a replacement, but by this time I never wished to see the interior of that little theatre again. I replied that since the work was such an ensemble piece it was impossible to rehearse with a third of the family missing and we should call it a day until the man was replaced. The next day, and with the greatest relief, I fled Brussels.

New York, 1988

I first met Mischa B. in New York where Lars Schmidt, my French producer, introduced us and we got on well immediately. Fortunately, having Coriolanus on at the time made me feel quite good, since the production was extremely visual and underpinned with a tremendous physical vocabulary and I would not feel awkward about Mischa seeing it. He eventually did see it and liked it and even admired the way Christopher Walken walked through his part. He liked the underplaying. Chris Walken had this way of underplaying so much that there was a danger of losing the play. It's an American trick to coast along real cool and then spear a big one which, by contrast to the rest, makes the audience sit up

with a jolt; at the same time you are demonstrating that you have the big
punch within you but you are conserving yourself. I was glad Mischa saw
that and wouldn't see Metamorphosis *as just a lucky one-off. Mischa was*
to be the greatest performer I have ever worked with and yet he allowed
himself to be putty in the hands of the director.

Monday 2 November

A nightmare day and night. Yesterday, during the last run-through, I
took some pictures with my new flash but it distracted me during the
run and I felt utterly wasted, deadened and unenergized. I know that
in future I must take nothing that I think may give me a bit of a lift.
After rehearsal Yoko tells me that the cast are having dinner together
at a restaurant downtown. It turns out to be a café where you cook
your own way – you buy bowls of uncooked food and cook it on a
hotplate that sits in the middle of your table. The place is in a very old
part of Tokyo, where rows of low houses line both sides of the road in
which are tucked away smoky little cafés packed with customers. So
you get your bowl and empty the veg on to your hot plate, add cheese
and then some meat and chop it all up and stir it until it has the
consistency you wish and then scoop it up with tiny metal spatulas on
to your dish. The café is packed as we enter and of course my warped
mind sees it as a marvellous photo opportunity. The café is too small
for the intrusion of such a bulky camera with a 200mm lens and Yuji,
the lodger, takes my bag with its contents, not knowing that my
bleeding, pulsating heart is in there. I am determined to photograph
this strange and wondrous place, but do not wish to make a deal out of
it and disturb the proceedings, and while I chatter lightly, like a
demented parrot squawking away, my mind is wondering when the
opportunity will easily and casually present itself. So I gabble, '*Oyishi,
totemai oyishi*' (delicious, very delicious), hoping to elicit some degree
of approval.

Mari sits on my right, Amon opposite with his vitality always
bubbling and the energetic, intense Atsuko next to him. They are so
unlike their British counterparts once they leave rehearsal. They
squeal with laughter at everything, but of course are feeling high from
a non-stop run. They joke, question, want to know other languages,
and ask me how Japanese sounds to me. Is it like Italian or French? I
say really it is like no other language on earth but might, I venture
(correctly I think), resemble Hebrew. So they ask for an example and

I say, 'How are you' in Hebrew, trying to sound very Japanese, and then they all do perfect imitations, so it does have a smidgen of Japanese.

I think that to get this picture I will have to go from 35mm to 200mm and I keep trying to see us as real life and not just as a photograph, but what the hell, I am in Japan and why not take a snap of my colleagues in this extraordinary, steamy, smoky café where everyone sits round hotplates, chopping and stirring their pancakes?

Yuji now makes up his pancake, then divides it into slices and quickly wolfs it down. He never drinks and his face has the clearest unlined expression of innocence. He amuses Atsuko with his delightful animal impersonations. Suddenly, in an act prompted by some loosening effect of the pancake and beer, and seeing my heavy bag lying there as if full of cocaine for a drug-starved addict, I walk casually to it, determined, now we have moved to a larger table, to take a picture by the door where I can get the whole group in shot. I tug at my camera which is wedged in with rehearsal papers that I have had to clear from my desk. I get it out and am prompted to go the whole hog and rescue my flash equipment and fasten it on, but meanwhile I take a couple of flashless snaps at low speed since it is reasonably light in there.

Yoko gets up now and says she'll take some so I can be in them and of course there is the usual bunching together of bodies whenever someone takes a photo. Snap! And then the group expands with beams of joy. I think, sod it, and fish down in my bag for the demon. I will not let it dominate my life deep in the unconscious of my dark bag in the small café. So I rummage in my bag and in my sweaty, exalted moment I attach the beast, the flash unit, to the top of the camera and now there it is in my hand . . . the time bomb! I slide it on to the camera 'shoe' and switch it on. The light is pulsing. No need to wait, like my small Olympus camera, for endless seconds for the flash to come between shots. I quickly change my speed from 1/30th to 1/250th of a second and it's all primed up and ready to go. So there I am in the centre of my fantasy and obsession in downtown Tokyo, using the flash for what I have dreamed about. I take a couple and then Yoko a couple and they all contract and expand and enjoy the moment since this will be our memory.

For once I have allowed my desire to surface. . . not just work, eat, sleep, but indulge in some whim. Perhaps those mechanical toys when abroad represent some degree of loneliness, perhaps an object can actually double as a friend. I've carried cameras all my life. Perhaps my obsession with the flash attachment exposes something, the desire to take night rather than day. Day is crowds, people at a distance, markets, back streets, landscapes, but night is personal.

I go home elated with the evening and like a little beetle return to my room glowing with excitement with my tiny conquest. I am Gregor Samsa who cuts out an advertisement of a lady in a fur muff and puts it in a picture frame that he has made himself. Kafka must have observed this somewhere in some house or other he visited, where some young child or youth had cut out a glamorous lady in a staid but somehow alluring ad and put it on the wall. Of course, it is intended to arouse our feelings of pity for one whose aesthetic needs are so pathetically simple.

Dream

I am in hospital being treated, I think, for a mild case of . . .? and instead I am injected, trussed up and abused. The black nurse examines my ear for wax and thrusts her long fingernail sharply into it. I squeal and say I've had enough and wish to discharge myself. I find my leg has been straightened out on a board as if plastered. I remove the dressing and see they have placed all sorts of contraptions like wire and coils behind the knee. And on top, thin slices of cooked meat and other vegetables. I must try to analyse what this means. Finish John Carey's book and then fall asleep.

Monday 2 November (happy again)

After last night's peccadillo, decide to have a long walk among the narrow back streets of Ginza and find the most beautiful coffee shop. It's called Pronto and it's small with little wooden tables, high stools and yellow stipple-painted walls, and they sell mostly cakes and delicate, inventive sandwiches. My spirits are uplifted just from being in here, since there is an atmosphere which suggests a bit of a special clientèle, or the thinking crowd. As I sit here I think what a handsome race the Japanese are. Some of them possess the most sensitive features, dark eyes, sharp noses and sensuous mouths and in fact frequently put me in mind of Kafka's face with his jet-black hair and penetrating eyes – he could have been taken for a Japanese himself.

Had dinner Saturday with a garlicky Aussie woman who was a

friend of a friend and she remarked that the Japanese tend to lead rather single lives and have few friends, which seemed to go completely against what I have observed, and yet in the month I have been here I have noticed that the cast are private with their relationships. In London you would generally observe a friend of the actor or a spouse turn up or even wish to see a run-through; here I have seen none. So it is possible that the work life and personal life are kept distinctly apart, which is no bad thing. I find I can't always bear those wives who crawl around watching their adored husbands at every possible rehearsal.

Here they like to keep their relationships private, which is also refreshing since my relationship with the actors and theirs with me are quite intense and intimate for a short period of time and there must be implicit trust. I have an old-fashioned belief that the company are a unique team, a kind of surrogate family, and when on tour I have found that spouses break up this harmony, although I can see they are necessary for some and can alleviate loneliness in others. Also having the spouse along gives an opportunity for a holiday in some exotic places.

Curiously, I find that most actors I know have less than interesting partners, or is it merely that I find some of them unpalatably dreary, devoid of the vitality of the actor? Is it jealousy? Or is it simply that volatile and creative performers often choose dreary spouses to create some calmness in the house? This is more likely.

So here in Japan you see no one. You are, as far as they are concerned, married to them for this period of time. Their wives, boyfriends, husbands stay at home and wait, and they seem to be much happier this way. I haven't even met Susumi's wife: she was not invited along for the weekend at the hot springs, nor has she seen a run, although you might think he would have been proud to have her see what, after all, is his production. Last night when the actors went out, they brought no one else. They seem only to know each other and this confirms what the Aussie says. Somehow the population grows but they don't seem to marry, have kids or many friends. All the company are single and when I see the men leave the offices at night they get merry, stagger round the streets and then flop home on the last tube.

Tuesday 3 November

Getting bored with my second month in one year in Tokyo and distressed with the bad costumes; so far not very good lights either, but things will improve since we have a week in the theatre! I walked round yesterday with Yoko as a reward and decided to try out a charming little sushi bar I have seen in a back street, Azuma Street, off Ginza. Everything is off Ginza once you see the size of it. We enter and it is empty. Elegant, wooden, small and cosy. We are greeted with enthusiasm and seated with aplomb. Our dishes are tastefully presented. The owner is smiling and chatting about how he once worked in Washington, where he learned to speak English, and his apprentice assistant is grinning and asking if I'm a yakusha (actor), since all they seem to watch in Japan is the wretched Rambo. (It was even playing in my local gym as I was doing my physical jerks; I could see myself pretending to be a Russian commandant and I looked guiltily round the gym to see if anyone had sussed, but they all kept on pumping away.)

Meanwhile the evening deepens into night and the grey suits of Japan are choking the streets of Ginza and I wonder what to eat next and order a tiny salad of cress and cucumber. I am not *so* hungry, having done no real work for days, it seems. I wish I had, as I did once in LA, just directed the play and split. I had only ten days to lay the foundations of my play *Greek*, since a tour of *Hamlet* had been arranged for when I came back, so I had to work fast and it was finished and on the nose in ten days. The lights and set I left to them and they did it well, and there was none of that hanging around when you have arrived early at your destination and have to while the time away with endless runs and bitty notes.

The bill eventually comes, wreathed in smiles and thank yous, and although we have together consumed no more than ten tiny pieces of fish and one sake, the bill is 12,000 Yen which is over sixty pounds! The charm, the small talk, the smiles, the cloying 'are you an actor', and even my concern that the place was empty (I now see why) - all this freezes in my stomach in the face of such naked theft. I do something very unusual apparently, given the protocol that exists here, and ask for a breakdown. They have to work it out retrospectively to make the food fit the bill. They try to itemize it to make it come out at the price, but it is obviously a great strain and they have to keep consulting each other until they eventually make it fit.

Go home and sleep and re-read *A Clockwork Orange*, since Susumi is passionate about staging it in Japan. It would stage well, since the language is so gorgeous and that element was lost in the film, let alone the version that was attempted by the RSC some while ago as a musical!

I'm sitting in a café opposite the Saison Theatre, looking straight down Ginza Street, and can feel the shadows of the *Salomé/Trial* company, since this is where they used to come for coffee and sit by the window and chat. I can still sense their presence.

Carrying on with *A Clockwork Orange*, I feel increasingly that a wonderful play is inside this book. I will shape a play out of *CO* as soon as possible – after all, it was one of the inspirations for *East*.

Wednesday 4 November

Suddenly the play is getting bad as far as the lighting is concerned. This is a key element of the show and it bothers me so much that I decide to put my personal life on hold. I realize my life shouldn't revolve around an incompetent technician, although I have known from my first meeting with him that there would be problems because of his loose, casual attitude. Should no longer be a one-man band and do too much myself, but must always have my own technicians flown in whenever the production is ready, as Robert Wilson does when staging *Einstein on the Beach*.

All this is a pain in the arse and just to rub salt in the wound I see Sir Colin Davis come to breakfast, all calm and beaming with his wife. I even feel humiliated sitting here alone day after day.

Simplify the light – start with open white light until the mood of the play changes and this will have the greater effect. A quick lighting rehearsal with cast, light the bloody actors swiftly and then run it. Be daring. Use silhouette. Let the images of the actors do it and let the movement be seen, and their acting. Bang the lights up startlingly as the chief clerk enters, revealing them raw and naked, exposed in their domesticity. When he exits and they say, 'Oh God', bring lights down to their stools, revealing them as small creatures in their tiny islands of light. Each family member separated from the next by a lake of darkness.

Sir Colin conducts very good Mozart, apparently.

Japanese women are beautiful and very sexy.
Just walking down Ginza High Street I see

A field of black tulips swaying in the breeze,
Their chiselled-out lips and cat-like noses
Beneath a pair of moony dark-brown eyes.
They sway, black-suited, brushed by jet-black hair
That waterfalls straight, their black stockings tear
Along wide Ginza Street, like Kabuki heroines
Who always insist on dying for their men

Years ago I used to have a penchant for playing with lights and dabbling with all the pretty colours, but now I have learned that the less the better. My lights were a light show and often, I thought, rather beautiful, but sometimes the audience would come out whistling the light cues. Now I light everything in white or the great amber.

Wednesday 4 November, 5 p.m.
After the gym feel marginally better but now will be disappointed if I cannot share this experience since everything here seems so fascinating and the greatest desire is to show and share it with someone close to you. Greta's costumes are now excellent and Mother's gigantic hairdo outrageous but also marvellous, hideous, surreal. The lodger looks perfect and punk-like. Dad looks a little dreary since there is nothing being said here and no statement made. When I get into the theatre, as if by reflex action my stomach and side begin to pain me. However, it all looks very good now with the improvements and I have a whole week to keep polishing. So the relief is acute and the show begins to look once again like the familiar friend I once knew.

Not been feeling so ill for years, what with all the stress and decisions, and I think I have been raving a bit about the bad lights and costumes, but it's all getting slowly better and I must try to control any sense of frustration.

Thursday 5 November
I am sweaty with deprivation. Deprived of a witness to my work here in Japan. Yesterday in the theatre there were more lamps than I have ever seen, courtesy of Mitsubishi. We have lamps for every possible combination and permutation, and yet the best lighting effect in the entire show is achieved with a solitary powerful lamp that sits on stage right at the front and throws a giant silhouette on the backcloth. We therefore see both the giant shadows of the characters on the screen

and their faces strongly, albeit fiercely, lit. It still works beautifully when the father appears to crush the son in silhouette and yet Mr Samsa is merely sitting on his stool. Even the technicians laugh when he slowly sits and the poor beetle appears to be crushed flat. It is one of those extraordinary bonuses that can happen when all the elements seem to be working for you and one of them will produce an unexpected gift. Again, the same one lamp is used when Greta and her mother go to empty Gregor's room. It throws their shadows on to a screen and the giant black shapes seem to form a parallel to the nightmare and intensify the action like a Greek chorus of giants. The staff at the Sphere all watch fascinated and while it has far fewer tricks than *Einstein on the Beach*, our piece, I must modestly say, has far more power and heart.

The next stage is to make sure that the light forges with the music and the text. The lighting 'designer' wishes to impose his ideas on to it but these cannot begin to compare with what has been accumulated over ten productions and trial and error, the gradual building and elimination of waste, the streamlining and then the discovery that all the best ideas come by accident. It was a quirk of fate that since originally we did not know what to put behind the set we just left it as it was with the cyclorama. In Tokyo we back-light the giant cyclorama in blue and the women then play their scene out only in silhouette, with their bodies extended and the fingers stretched and clawing the air – I have seen nothing so beautiful or commanding. They have the quality of Victorian cut-outs or Christmas cards. The silhouette highlights what they are feeling as well as what they say. The language of the body has never been so clearly stated as when the mother pleads with the daughter to let her see her son. The lighting reminds me of painting; it seems to have the explosions of a Goya at times; then sometimes a calm serenity like Magritte and then again it reminds me of a Fritz Lang film. The facsimile steel beetle hangs over the family, doubling as a roof before it is filled in and the skeletal structure throws shadows over the screen as Greta 'opens' the door. This effect again is done with only two lights crossing each other on stage. The criss-cross effect creates a nightmare vision as if the interior of Gregor's room were seen from the beetle's point of view . . . distorted, hideous and fragmented. When Greta closes the door life normalizes again, but for a few seconds we have a sense of what it must be like for Gregor. Light does this in a way that words could never do.

Mari's hair seems to be growing at each rehearsal. It is the weirdest I have ever seen, it completely dominates her and yet she carries it off. It's almost obscene, something perversely Victorian, a lady whose repressed sexuality finds its outlet in the most bizarre of hairdos. Perhaps those elaborate hairstyles were the result of having little power in society except over your fashion. Atsuko also has her hair up but in a less exaggerated way, as if she were an apprentice mother. Yuji, the lodger, has his hair combed straight up in the air. What all these hairstyles do is to create an effect of energy, bizarre power, freedom, eccentricity and self-absorption. Also something a little perverted, erotic, onanistic. The father now needs attending to so as not to be totally over-haired by his wife.

Yesterday I was terribly moved by a simple impression that was partly created by the light and partly by Gregor. The scene where Gregor hears a fly and eventually puts out a digit, captures it and then chews it is usually the sign of his irrevocable slide into insect spirit and the diminishing of human values, as milk has now been traded for flies. After he has his late supper, so to speak, we slowly lower the light on his poor dehumanized shape while increasing the blue cyclorama as the atmosphere of night pervades the scene. As the fade starts you see this sad silhouette of Gregor and the form of mother and father leaning against the pole like some strange cocoon. Then I ask Amon to open up his body by thrusting his arm out and slowly to climb the frame. Straddling it with his feet and hands on each side and back-lit, he looks exactly like some gigantic 'thing', inhuman, monstrous, and then he becomes quite still and stays like that for about fifteen seconds. So nothing happens for an eternity of fifteen seconds. By this we seem to sense that this is Gregor's life for ever or until he dies. To sleep like this, almost a great spider straddled over the frame as if it were a web and just the faint sound of the wind engulfing his terrible loneliness while others sleep in soft, warm beds and hold each other – Gregor's life is destined to be thus. Frozen there, his silhouette is truly a sad and terrible image to leave on the retina of the audience. Then we see the family, the sad lumps of the mother, father and Gregor in the centre. The parents feel that they have inherited a strange monster that fills their hearts and souls with shame. I imagine this must be the kind of guilt felt by the mother of a deformed or handicapped child while she enviously regards the perfectly formed limbs of others' children.

The image of the family sleeping under one roof also put me in mind of a photo taken by Diane Arbus, the highly sensitive recorder of the underlife of New York's working classes. It is a poignant picture of a Jewish lower-middle class family in their Brooklyn apartment. The lounge in which the picture was taken is similar to my mother's, a three-piece suite, large sofa, two armchairs, coffee table, etc. Except that in the New York version there is a plastic shade on the lamp, I believe. The father looks like a normal angst-ridden Jewish manager of a chemist shop or men's store and his wife stays home, but what distinguishes this family group from all others is that amidst this deadening and rigid normality is the gigantic presence of the son. He is a huge, overgrown monster of over eight and a half feet, and his head is stooped so as not to hit the ceiling. He leans on a walking stick and has a support shoe on one foot. He looks weak from his efforts to carry such a weight and yet he has a thick head of hair and seems quite virile in other aspects.

What is astonishing about the photo of the gentle giant is the way the mother and father are posed, as if everything were quite normal, and there are covers protecting the furniture from getting soiled. The father has one hand in his jacket and looks full of concealed grief, while the mother stares up, hands on her hips. They even have a repro painting on the wall with a top light over it as if it were an old master. It's a painfully moving study of a bourgeois family reacting as might the Samsa family to the ultimate horror happening to them.

For a Jewish family, for some inexplicable reason, it seems all the more a hideous and uncalled-for curse. Why? In a gentile family perhaps they would be a little proud of the freak . . . put him in a circus or side-show or at least not feel so deeply *responsible*! But for those burdened with the guilt of being of a faith that has for so long been cursed, it is surely an outward sign of their degeneracy. One of the lamps in the photo stands next to an electric clock which has the time 11.10. I presume it's p.m., since the windows look black, and I wonder how Diane Arbus came to stay so late. The people who have in their charge such an unfortunate creature must carry this woe and agony in their hearts all their lives and in every waking minute. What a terrible cross to bear.

So all in a trice, seeing this awful immobile lump seeking the sweetness of sleep just like anyone else seems to strike many chords. After fifteen seconds we fade the blue down and it seems to leave an after-image on the retina. We continue until 9.30 p.m., have some sushi with the directors of Sphere and then, with my stomach in knots, I come home.

Friday 6 November

Beautiful morning. I go for a walk. In a languid mood wander into a shop and try on a Ralph Lauren suit which I think rather suits me; suddenly feel like Richard III prating about getting some tailors to adorn his form. The suit is 180,000 Yen, which seems a trifle high (over £900) but it is an elegant three-piece. Then I wander out and float in the morning sunshine, relaxing and easing out the five weeks of solitary work. The show looks very good, but the technical time has taken away some of the acting thrust and we must get back to it now. Even look forward to going in and having a cappuccino where a startlingly beautiful girl works in the bar opposite the theatre. She is bright, enchanting, speaks perfect English and is a huge fan of Sarah Brightman, whom she resembles in a Japanese way. She has a powerful-looking, athletic body and a clear skin – Japanese women can be really exquisite.

The theatre complex with hotel, restaurants, bars, shops, has lots to occupy a drifter. Later I will have a sushi in one of the three sushi bars after watching the unravelling of one of the most beautiful shows on earth . . . at least to me.

The actors are now established in their dressing rooms, their little surrogate homes for the next month. They begin, like birds, to make nests of them and make them feel more homely. Mari has her cassette deck playing and her small fold-away mobile phone at the ready. Masumi has a large silk curtain over the door so that he can leave the door open and still be masked off, and he has a fridge filled with beers. This time, before the first performance when the actors are ensconced in their trenches, is one of the most significant times in the theatre, since it is a building time when you start adding that invisible skin, that extra layer that allows you to go on to that stage. This tiny room is your second home, sanctuary, escape hole and it can also be terribly depressing as you sit there and wait. If you arrive early the minutes ache their way by, since each minute is a heavier minute than the civilian minute. You might answer letters, try to read the paper, stare at yourself, inspecting the terrain as if you were looking for some hints of erosion since the night before. It's also a condemned cell, the last station of the cross and the last place you are in before you go out in front to be fried, executed by a thousand eyes and shot down in flames by the critics. The interval is sweet repose, your hot cuppa waiting for you, and a lie-down. The end is best, when you enter this room after a show and you have shed the sweat, the pain and the fear and replaced them with exhilaration, the curtain down and the applause. The exit from the stage usually through a heavy pass door, up some stairs and yes, it's over. Sheer sweet bliss!

The slow run-through went well yesterday: the lighting now looks as beautiful as a dream and all the cues work. This is after sixteen hours of painful refocusing. Now as the cues unroll with perfect efficiency, the show reveals itself in a series of exquisite events. It is breathtaking, seeing it for the first time in this beautiful new auditorium. This music is now superior to anything I have had on stage before for this play. The sound system is perfect and everything is in balance, no element dominating. There are explosions of movement and moments of utter stillness. When Gregor is first seen, that frenzied, frantic bursting all over the stage as if the cast had been electrocuted is extraordinary, for in the centre of all this madness sits Gregor as still as a rock. He then moves an inch at a time, small, infinitely minuscule movements which nevertheless cause a tremor in the cast. It is one of my best inventions and I enjoy watching it each time. Masumi still looks distant from the style of the others and perhaps now, in costume, even more so since the women's stylized hairdos make them look quite incredible and yet in an archly Victorian manner, while Masumi has achieved a fluffed-up look that gives an impression of an ageing teddy boy. The run feels a little expanded and even a bit bloated, lasting nearly two hours without an interval. The ending is rather moving and simple and our electrician has rigged up a cold blue light which seems to cast an unearthly glow over Gregor's death as his body gradually folds itself like the corpse of an insect. Since it is the first complete run it is very exciting and all the staff are there, from the various producers. I am relieved to see the old monster reborn. In Japan.

North Carolina, 1988/New York, 1989

When we tried out the show in Duke's University, North Carolina, it was to give Mischa a good head start in his first ever stage play. It was a gruelling four weeks for him in this quiet town, but he loved working at it and feeling his voice getting stronger each day. Never was anyone so dedicated as he sat in the bar of the Duke's Hotel with a small cigar but refusing any alcohol during the run, and yet he liked the odd tipple.

I loved the early mornings and I would come downstairs for breakfast before anyone else, particularly the actors, so I could sit, write and stare out of the window on to a picture-postcard, snow-covered world, sheer blue, wide-open sky and wintry trees, fields rolling away to endless horizons. I would savour my American breakfast which is like no other breakfast in the world since it tastes of innocence, simplicity, openness and Norman Rockwell country. The endless coffee, toasted bagel and cream cheese, and then I'd wander into the old town. Each night Mischa would ask me how it went. He was a passionate worker who would turn up hours before anyone else and work out.

So we arrived in New York in the winter of 1989, one hundred years after the gold rush. January is a crisp time to be in New York – you wrap your overcoat round your body like a bandage, so the buttonholes overtake the buttons, and you fall into a steamy coffee shop at the earliest opportunity. The show had its première and there was more than the usual assortment of glitterati since this was the night of nights when the world's great darling – defector, beautiful dancer, myth, Russian – was to make his début in Kafka, the scripture of the intelligentsia, and so it was Kafka, Baryshnikov and Berkoff on Broadway. A strange mix, you might say.

From the stretch limos stepped Diana Ross, Nancy Reagan, David Bowie, etc. They were all watching, with only minor adjustments, the same creation I had put together in that hot little church in Islington all those years ago, a story that Kafka wrote seventy years before that, a tale of brilliant invention, written in exquisite detail. It reminds one of a Japanese print, or a fairytale about a frog who changes into a prince but needs to be loved to effect this change. So Kafka's need for his father's love and approval may have led to his symbolic change into the loathsome bug, a parasite, for that is how he liked to imagine his father saw him. Could the beetle wake up one morning and find that it has all been a nasty dream? Someone needs to kiss Gregor Samsa, but then we might not have one of the great stories of all time. Kafka sold few copies of his books but seventy years after his death we saw his simply written and carefully wrought novella on Broadway with stretch limos sliding to a halt outside the Barrymore, like long black beetles depositing their dung.

In the final analysis nothing will ever compare to the story, but then it provides fuel and inspiration for a piece of phantasmagorical theatre and we can't always be entertained by The Three Sisters. The huge throngs of

126

young people that excitedly filled the Mermaid Theatre in London in 1986 suggest that there is very much a desire, if not a need, for this kind of theatre. So that night on Broadway was filled with a galaxy of celebs, and I watched from the bar across the street as the prestige first-nighters came to pay homage not to Kafka but to Mischa and Broadway.

What did Nancy Reagan say to her husband? 'Hey, I saw this weird play about a guy who changes into a bug.' 'Really, Nancy, didn't Spielberg make a movie of it?' In the chill, critical, or rather non-critical, atmosphere of New York such works aren't really to the taste of those raised on the corn-feed of realistic Yankee drama and Neil Simon, worthy as these plays may be. So the production was not only dismissed, it was shat upon, vilified, and yet still managed to pack the house. New York reviewers isolated themselves by being the only city to give this show the thumbs down. After Paris, Sydney, Düsseldorf, London, Tokyo, Tel Aviv, New York proved to be the oddball. And I hasten to add that it is not because the Americans are more alert, avant garde, cosmopolitan or intelligent! Rather brutish materialism has corroded the optic nerve which appears within. Or has materialism created a need to see things that support their hunger for facts: what is real? Real humans discussing real things.

I recall a play that was a big Broadway hit, Six Degrees of Separation. *In the first scenes every other sentence is concerned with money, the need for it or the lack of it, and the audience chuckled sympathetically with the characters' 'plight' and smiled benignly as they mentioned the brand names that acted on their consumer-addled brains like Pavlovian dogs that salivate at the sound of a bell. This is an area that Molière deals with in* Le Bourgeois Gentilhomme, *but that was and is a masterpiece, and we laugh at Molière's creations with their money-orientated values, whereas in the other piece the audience are persuaded to be sympathetic with the characters' nauseous lifestyle.*

Anyway, at least I tried to assemble around Mischa the best cast of actors I could find so that he should believe that my profession had high artistic standards. René Auberjonois, whom I saw give a stunning Richard III at the Mark Taper Forum in LA years ago, played Dad and was brilliant. Laura Esterman, who was so unforgettable in Kvetch, *played Mrs Samsa and quite superbly too, and a new actress called Madeleine Potter was very good as Greta and highly professional. So we had a first class cast.*

On the evening of that première we all gathered in a hotel room after the ritualistic drinks in Sardi's. Lars Schmidt, the European producer, Roger Stevens, the great doyen of the American theatre, and collected wives plus one or two others had a light supper, congratulated each other on the reception, which was ecstatic, cooed over how marvellous Mischa had been, etc., etc. We had the TV on to hear the middling-to-good TV critics and then Lars, whom I had not noticed go out suddenly, made an appearance wearing the longest face I have ever seen him wear as he entered the room with the New York Times *under his arm. The review from the current scribbler, Frank Rich, was not just bad – it was full of vitriol and rank stupidity. I looked at these men of power, experience, wealth and culture hovering around this little turd of a review. Sniffing it, examining it, hoping it might even change as they stared at it. If New York, like London, had half a dozen daily papers, this reviewer would not have such prominence. But in New York one paper, one solitary paper, has the power to hurt and kill your show. How can they call this a democracy? Of course, there are two other papers that are not read by anyone who ever went to a theatre in their lives and as often as not have only three big words on the front page. However, they are far better in quality and more grown-up than their British counterparts. If they showed tits in a family paper, the paper would be burnt down by powerful feminist groups who would rightly declare that they were not cattle or whores to be ogled by leering yobs.*

Anyway, all the cast came in for dim praise or criticism, but the most banal statement of all time and what for me relegated Mr Rich's mind to the garbage heap of history, the dustbin of redundant journalism, was the review of the fine actor René Auberjonois in which his performance was compared to my *performance as Hitler in* War and Remembrance *(incidentally highly praised), as if I had chosen to model René's rôle on mine as Hitler!! And the junky critic seized on this performance to clout my actor. I had directed René as a bullying, oppressive father who eventually tries to kill his own son, but the raging had a certain satiric edge – he was more of a bullying buffoon, though his rages were also meant to terrify.*

Lars put the blame at my feet rather than with the cultural and artistic moribundity of the New York theatre and this individual critic. Notwithstanding, there was a huge amount of excitement for the play – the advance was a million dollars and business was running at $250,000 per week! This dropped after a few weeks to a respectable $150,000, but Mischa was getting sick of playing eight times a week, the mandatory number that performers should rebel against since it kills off all good actors.

He opted to close the limited season three weeks early, and who could blame him? To do that show twice a day for someone like Mischa must have been a killer.

He wasn't used to coasting through a matinée as many actors do. As a dancer, he was trained to give his all each moment he was on stage. I watched the performance a few times and went backstage with the odd note, but after a while you cannot watch any more when a show is on. It even depressed me to walk down 47th St to the Barrymore. I just liked the idea of a young Marlon Brando coming in here to prepare for his rôle in A Streetcar Named Desire *. . . New York is full of memories.*

Saturday 7 November

Here in Japan the actors are doing just four weeks of performances at this theatre since the Mitsubishi Corp. are not into making profits but want to circulate the best theatre in the world. They wish to buy art. Today the press and sponsors are taking a peek at the dress rehearsal and so I must try and trim it. It has grown somewhat.

Yesterday's run was very good. My mind is clear and focused on the issues at hand and we improve about a dozen small events. Like a motor needing a fine-tuning after its initial trial run which heats it up and expands its metal, the show needs tightening up. There are dozens of photographers in for the dress rehearsal and it feels as if we are at the inauguration of some huge and important event. It is only a few weeks ago that I watched the same group of photographers at the same theatre for *Einstein on the Beach*. There is the vibration of Einstein's name in the title, sounding powerful, like iron, like stone, like a heavy Jewish mystic, scientist, magician, and then the word beach. Cosy, down to earth, American, like, 'Don't let's get fazed by the genius Einstein, let's take him down to the beach.' There were many beautiful images in the Wilson production, but the sight of this dancer, dressed in white pants and white shirt, minimalistic uniform, striding forwards and backwards, was the silliest thing I have ever seen on a stage and acutely embarrassing in its devoted gaucheness. There are some things that are so *American*. Wilson seems to find some extraordinary virtues in repetition which, while working breathtakingly at times, in Glass's music, look merely silly in live actors. Let's get back to basics. There are some mime artists who impersonate technology in their street acts. One of their shticks is to perform video playbacks or when a video is stuck like a record and repeating itself. This is brilliant and one might find it necessary sometimes to return to the boardwalk or street to see real experimental artists. Anyway, our run-through works well and the feeling as the curtain slowly lifts like a skirt revealing the naughties underneath is exhilarating. I am astonished at how beautiful and Japanese it all looks. An ivory grey stage with black lines going to infinity. A light cyclorama emitting the faintest glow. The light for the first scene perfectly flat and even. It recalls Magritte or Chirico, the figures as surreal and potent as a Victorian waxwork.

Mr and Mrs Samsa and Greta remain totally frozen as if they were figures in a book waiting for volts of life to ignite them. Gregor walks up to his sister and they remain together during the opening scene, like a pose for an old-fashioned photo, each facing front. It looks startling and beautiful and Mrs Samsa's hair, which has now grown into a giant pompadour, has a sinister quality of old, dusty houses, aspidistras and emotions fiercely held in check by the intensity of the hair . . . aah, it is pure Dali! Yes, focus on one aspect of the being in which the personality has taken *refuge*. The cartoonist does this automatically, as if by reflex, and the British Gerald Scarfe is a master of it. So Mother and Father sit in this empty landscape waiting to be activated by Gregor's words . . . 'I have to work to keep them' . . . both Mother and Father come to life in joyful acceptance of his statement. Mr Samsa becomes a moustache-twirling old macho and so the two are manipulated by Gregor's words as if the words were strings to a puppet.

Then we see Gregor perform his daily chores as a continuous walk to the beat of the metronome. He keeps looking at his watch as if time was a thread that ran through his life. I was fascinated by this piece of performance artistry when staying in LA and observing the young street artists. I recall a young black American whose imagination and technique were so beautiful I could have watched him for hours. He made himself into a living sculpture and fulfilled Oscar Wilde's prophetic credo that life copies art, for this is what was happening. While actors impersonate real people, this performer and thousands like him were using movies, music, videos, machinery, and extending the art of the performer in every direction. So Amon tries this and does it well, using his round, innocent face and large brown eyes, and is for the Japanese the perfect Gregor. I have always been lucky with Gregors!

In this introduction to the play, the light has changed to three areas as each member of Gregor's family fulfils his or her function like dutiful puppets of their environment, Mother sewing beautifully, Father smoking his evening cigar and drinking a beer, Greta studying her French. The scene satisfies . . . it is a painting of tranquillity and contentment brought to life. I sit back and relax and know it's working; there is a balance between the visual, textual and musical. The three are perfected, wedded and dependent on each other now, like a triad. As fused and as related to each other as the libretto and music in an opera.

As Gregor finishes his scene with his sister and walks back to his bed from whence he will never return as a human, his family sing out, 'Goodnight, Gregor', in a kind of threnody, elongating his name until it disappears. The blue light of night has now abruptly changed to a fierce white light of day, but the family are still isolated within their spheres as if they were being scrutinized under a microscope. Now the timing speeds up as the family perform the daily rituals of eating their breakfast, still in perfect synchronicity and stopping the beat from time to time as they wonder what has happened to Gregor who normally would have been up at an ungodly hour. When they stop for a moment and express concern they become human, worried individuals, but when reassured that the alarm clock was set and all is in order they continue on their mechanical way.

Another gift to this scene derived from a mistake that occurred when the family turn on their stools, calling Gregor to get up, spinning like frantic spools of cotton. They are meant to stop in unison but one day Mari forgot and continued for another cycle. Now this is part of her character in that she flutters more than the others and she executes the last turn beautifully, like a flamenco dancer. One is rewarded by mistakes.

Suddenly there are three loud knocks and the chief clerk is on the stage. And so the play unfolds itself, each scene linking with the next and each character integrated into the weft and warp of the action and with the others. The music now binds it all and I watch without trepidation and without boredom. I am able to sit and observe and let all the memories float beneath this experience as if they were a series of palimpsests upon which new engravings are continually being written.

I am sitting next to Yoko, who rapidly and with tremendous efficiency takes down my few notes. For this first dress rehearsal I am excited; I get cross if the sound or light isn't quite right but know I can adjust it. I again rejoice with the new-found image when Amon goes into his sleep position against the deep Van Gogh starry night and looks like a poor sad thing hanging in space. I look forward to these highlights intensely and am doubly rewarded when a stranger who has never seen it comes in or when the producer Susumi comes by. But his English is not so good and so he generally says, 'Velly niiice!'

I watch the play intensify its drama. The beetle escapes when the father is absent from the house and for the first time seeks freedom from his claustrophobic prison. Then Mr Samsa returns unexpectedly and Gregor is pounded with apples thrown by his furious father. The play continues and is firming up, coalescing and binding until there will be no seams or joins. I now look forward to the lodger making his slow entrance and the ecstatic expression of Mrs Samsa as she computes all the possibilities of this new man and then the gradual eroding of those dreams as we see what a beast he is. I watch the drunken lodger dragging the family on to the floor for the frenzied dance when Greta is forced to play the violin for him. By deciding to play much of this dance in silhouette, as if draining them of the colour of life, we see them like poor ghost-like shades. Gregor hears all this and decides he can take no more; he invades the room using the only thing he can to protect them – his repellent ugliness. He wishes above all to protect Greta. Atsuko now *is* Greta. She is an Alice in Wonderland Greta. Her plaintive expression registers all there is to know about a young girl growing up and reacting to everything as if it were the most important thing in the world. Eventually the lodger can take no more of this disgusting family with their awful secret revealed and he exits cheekily, walking backwards, executing a moonwalk. The Samsas are alone with their grief and the poor, disgusting, dying Gregor on the floor in front of them. Hopelessness and despair are all they can look forward to. They scream silently, slowly stretching out their arms and letting out this imagined howl, the famous theatrical cliché of all time, but it works in this context and we see the three like a Greek chorus from Hades with that dark terrible hole in the middle of their faces. Echoes of Francis Bacon.

Greta alone manages to retain some semblance of sanity and the will to live. She makes them confront what she believes is the awful truth, that this creature is no longer her brother, that it is an evil creature who wants the whole apartment to itself and drives away their lodger. Thus she wilfully misinterprets all Gregor's good intentions . . . 'Of course it's not Gregor,' she insists. Is it a recommendation for euthanasia when the personality has faded? A shifting of responsibility for a declining old parent to the sanctuary of an old people's home? Throw out your unwanted. But Gregor cannot be sent anywhere and so opts to die peacefully and serenely while thinking of this family with the affection he used to know. His death brings the family back to a renewed surge for life. It becomes suddenly a fertility play. The old god dies and a new one is born. Spring must come and death takes away the moribund. Seasons are represented by their anthropomorphic symbols. The sun will shine today and the Samsas' deepest wish is to get on a bus and ride into the open country with the sunshine flooding the windows. Did Kafka have this desire when working in the oppressive workers' insurance building? Did he so many times gaze out of the window and long to take a bus into the open country? Greta becomes suddenly aware that her body is feeling the surges of maturity . . . Mr Samsa talks of a husband for her.

Mrs Samsa finishes the play with the final poignant line, 'The crocuses will just be coming out.' Life, growth, fertility, sexuality, marriage. All things Kafka denied himself as he sat in his room each day, writing and forever writing . . . a solitary existence . . . The curtain comes down on a good dress rehearsal and I say, '*Agrigato!*' (Thank you). 'It was a good run-through . . .'

Postscript

I've finished, more or less . . . Feel oppressed this morning and racked at every turn, so take myself to the gym and once on the treadmill feel better. Miraculously the pain disappears and works off, though as soon as I leave it returns. So I enter my favourite tea shop, Lipton's, and I sit and write and feel it's all over. Last night's party was over quickly and I went to bed early and watched CNN and Larry King live.

Go and buy myself a jacket to cheer myself up since I am growing ashamed of my solitary being at breakfast – I am eating my way into my journal like Kafka who, after eating his way through the fruits of life, started chewing the kernel and after that gnawed away at himself, peeling away the flesh like layers of onion until nothing existed except literature itself . . . the shadowy facsimile of life.

Sunday 8 November

Yet another run-through yesterday and I nearly fall asleep, since a week of dress rehearsal is just a tad too much, but the producers don't seem familiar with the process and hover round the show like flies round meat. Already the play is coming loose at the seams. It badly needs an audience to set it and to raise the level, like yeast on dough, or it will become flat and mannered. I now see things that are not interesting and I can hardly bear to watch it without suffering an intense stomach ache, as if raw juices of frustration were some harsh acid eating me away. I am becoming tired of the show and the people only because it has gone beyond its rehearsal time and is starting to curdle. I am even getting tired of the Seiyo Hotel, which is one of the world's best. I am suffering from overkill and maybe should visit Kyoto, where I have never been, or leave Japan altogether and stop in Bangkok. However, there are compensations in that I am writing and planning and looking forward to directing *Decadence* for my first movie.

Last night the lodger took us all to a bar run by Henry Miller's ex-wife. It is a charming place eight floors up in a suburb of Tokyo. She was only with Miller four years and was wife number eight. A kind of doll around the house. She gets up on the small stage and sings brilliantly. I love the sleazy, easy feeling of the club. She shows me some of Henry's paintings which she has up in the loo. I try to get some info on Henry, but she hasn't much to say. She probably didn't even know him that well and certainly never had sexual relations, since by that time he was only into ping-pong, which he played avidly. This will be my last Sunday, I think to myself with some satisfaction.

Monday 9 November

Yesterday was my first really nice day since I've been here. Like an English Sunday in Camden Lock. I speed through my solitary porridge and go with Yoko to Shinjuku, the vast shopping centre in central Tokyo. There is something really exhilarating about shopping on Sunday – it has a completely different atmosphere, as if it were a carnival or festival. After a week of slog it's a great entertainment to jump around the stores which for me become vast play areas as you leap from floor to floor. The streets are thronged with millions of people and the area has become mostly pedestrianized for the day. Some stores have exhibitions; there is one on Shakespeare through the eyes of painters throughout the ages. There is also one on Beardsley and the English School of book illustrators. I enjoy Beardsley exhibits and the delightful designs of Arthur Rackham and the delicate, charming world of children's books with their serene illustrations, so perfectly drawn, of country groves, bowers, misty mornings, dewy countrysides and pouting Alices. I even see a first edition of *Salomé* dated 1894 which I nobble immediately and with great satisfaction since I have been looking for one of those for years to add to my Oscar ephemera.

The clothes are the most inventive I have ever seen. We go to one of those stores which specializes in designer clothes and I spend an hour getting in and out of baggy pants, with Yoko helping me, looking on and advising. After all the exploring and the excitement of buying my precious book we end up in a café drinking coffee in a semi-delirium of delight, taking snaps and munching delicious childhood sandwiches served by pretty Japanese creatures. Then we take a taxi driven by the usual white-gloved driver to the Marji area, where the throngs are even more intense and the streets are packed with stalls and shoppers pouring like lava through every small, twisting, snaking back street, looking and prying. At last I find the street I have been looking for and have not seen in all the weeks I have been here, the place I will love most of all, the source of so much of my life and work and where the first shoots of the theatre start. The open air . . . the street or avenue in the park where the young performers come and strut their stuff. There is the most amazing proliferation of energy and innovation I have yet seen in Japan. An amazing sight to be had. And I am awed.

Now, sitting in my fave café in Ginza, the charming little Pronto, I am suddenly exceedingly happy and, of course, when you ebb and flow with the tide of humanity it must feed you. In the park yesterday was a detonation of energy the like of which I have only seen in Central Park, New York, and on the Boardwalk in Venice, LA. Certainly never in London, since there they ban street theatre and spontaneous activity in the parks. One actually has to audition to perform in the refined precincts of Covent Garden, unbelievable as this may seem! In the park in Tokyo there is a long avenue packed with every variety of human activity and I can only gape and gawp at the sight of the hairy underbelly of Japanese culture.

Groups of dancers, quiffed like cartoons of Elvis Presley, are executing perfect routines, tidal waves of jet-black hair perched, stiffened and intact over their pale faces, thin drain-pipe bodies, with matchstick legs disappearing into Cuban-heeled boots. They form a dance team in a circle all facing each other and leaping, gyrating, twisting, crouching, spinning, while opposite and a little further down, another group perform the most exacting routine of a dance version of martial arts. We walk on, taking in ever conceivable sight, drinking it in, since it is what I have heard about and yet nobody has taken me to see it. Pre-Raphaelite rock-star impersonators with flowing tresses dyed red are furiously impersonating Jagger and even improving on the original as the Japanese are wont to do. Their carmine-painted lips and flaring hair flowing in the wind make them look like exquisite dolls. We stroll on past the crowds of teeny-bopper girls who are going crazy for the doll-like painted naughty boys in their high-heeled boots and tight pants and then we see roller-skaters, young, lithe, handsome – or rather pretty, since Japanese men have an aesthetic delicacy missing from their heavier, fleshier Nordic counterparts. The skaters are gyrating and dancing in formation to music, bumping and grinding their hips, while an old lady looks on in shock. The park is packed with abandoned wild energy, a river flowing with flesh, and talented flesh at that, and with a real, urgent need to perform. The young, as usual, point the way, since they are abandoned, liberated and ecstatic in their discovery of their own skills. We eat some noodles by one of the many dozens of stalls that are steaming, chopping, cooking and sending their delicious aromas over the park. It is wonderful and just what I need after five weeks of *Metamorphosis*.

Tuesday 10 November

They laughed a lot last night at the first preview, at the irony of the piece and the quirks of human nature when confronted with the unacceptable. They laughed at the look of astonishment on the face of the mother as she gazes for the first time at the poor beast. They laughed at Gregor who, after he crawls arduously into the room, declaims that he will 'put his clothes on at once, pack his samples and be off', all in a squeaky voice. I think Kafka had a savage sense of humour and an exquisite feeling for irony. The show works well and the positions are sculptural and strong; the idea of the 'inner' person expressed through the body language is more delineated than ever before. I have almost completely rid the actors of that ugly naturalism in which you demonstrate your feeling in a bunched-up face which can scarcely be seen from the back of the theatre. Here they use their whole being to show what they feel, which of course not only can be seen at the back of the theatre but also creates another art form. When they have no words they can always be 'read'. More than ever I feel my work develop into a kind of school, not by rigid formula but by learning certain techniques which expand your ideology and communication skills. Also you might call it a socialist concept, since it is about the uniting of energy and the linking up of actors whose collected voices have more power and whose interaction with each other makes formidable visual and choreographic statements. Here we have duos and trios and even quartets. Sometimes they perform as if to music, and sometimes the forms of swirling bodies are stunning to watch. I feel that the audience is totally spellbound. Having the determination to make a form of ideology out of the actors and story leads one to keep finding inventions which heighten and highlight the story. For example, the deadly slow walk together as the family recall their past. This comes out of the mutilating of Gregor when Father pelts him with apples, one of which becomes embedded in his back and leads Gregor to wonder where on earth the old man got the energy for such violence. He recalls his ageing father as a limp, dependent old man being helped along by his two children on a Sunday outing.

There is a moment when they all sit staring into the distance and stretch their hands out as if warming them by the same fire, at the same time building a fire in their thoughts which eventually erupts. I thought the lighting technician would smirk at my naïveté, since I requested a deep red glow to come on at this point as if I was asking for blue for a cold day and yellow for a hot one, and yet as they stretch out their hands to the invisible fire their fingers appear to me as cats' claws. They make the innocent gesture we all made when children. Children of today can seldom experience the family sitting around the crackling hearth and shoving some more coal on and, while sitting there, allowing the flames to whisk them hypnotically into a meditative mood.

The family accuse each other but keep their eyes on the embers. It develops into a powerful scene as their faces become twisted with mutual hatred and they stare at their thoughts in the bloody embers. In their domestic arguments the flow of their words is affecting them as if they were gusts of wind and they are pushed backwards and forwards. That is so much more powerful to me than three bodies just sitting there, their mouths opening and shutting and a few stabbing gestures. The power of the group does not diminish the genius of the individual but rather enhances it as they become soloists and then ensemble players. This palpably made its effect on the invited audience last night. This style will not necessarily work with all plays, but a style or form should be found for each subject.

Bertolt Brecht also sought a method of expressing universal experience through what he defined as an alienation technique. I see this more and more clearly as his boredom with actors who impersonated life rather than expressing it dramatically. Not audience identification with an individual *but with the tragedy of humanity itself,* of which the audience is part. Turning the mirror back to them. That needs a subtle change in acting style so that the words become more emphatic and less naturalistic, the face more neutral and the body more versatile, always acting as a mask for the face.

When one wears a neutral Greek mask the smallest shift of emphasis in the body changes the expression on the stiff mask as the audience 'read' what they themselves like to imagine. So the audience participates and interprets. The use of instruments further heightens awareness, taking it out of the domestic and into the ritualistic. So the scenes of feeding Gregor, collecting the luggage from the lodger and throwing it into Gregor's room, the stamping of feet to force the escaping beetle back have now become almost dance-like imitations of life and thus comment on and parody an absurd situation. They have a curious beauty to them. I look forward to these 'moments' as areas in the play where the cast celebrate the action. In the same way the performers are larger than the rôles they play. When Greta explodes with an intense form of childlike frustration and embodies in her being the voice of a young teenage girl, almost pre-pubescent, she is all children. She symbolizes all neglected, frustrated children whose hearts explode with passion to express themselves, to organize, play the violin, be a ballet dancer or pianist. It is a performance on an epic scale, both individual and yet totally giving to the group's pattern of activities. Mind you, it is also terribly cute!

Wednesday 11 November

Last night I couldn't bear to see yet another run and so I took the camera in with some fast film and took photos. I pretend I am a theatre photographer but without a tripod they are bound to be a little soft focus.

Have lunch today with Martin Naylor who acts as a kind of impresario to the Japanese by suggesting to them companies to import. He is an utterly charming English businessman of the old school, yet lives in Japan, speaks fluent Japanese and is highly articulate about Japanese culture as well as British theatre. It's curious how different we are and yet I find I like being with people who are not 'arteests', are unpretentious and unfashionable, and yet give you better value for your time than those who are burdened with interpreting the world. I watch the show from the director's box along with Yuki, Yoko and the stage manager and it is distant from me since I am watching through the lens of my camera.

I am thinking now of leaving and when to go. Should I stop in Bangkok, the ejaculatory centre of the Eastern world? The idea of all those monstrous white businessmen tourists appals me, although I would like three days of swimming and warmth. But shouldn't I see Kyoto first? Or go straight back? I am invited to a dinner party where John Gielgud will be one of the guests and I am keen to be back for that so that I can tell him of the strange dream I had about him when sleeping in the hotel room in Paris where Oscar Wilde died such a violently unpleasant death in November 1900. I had been invited by Melvyn Bragg to give a small chat on the influence of French culture and its effect on the theatre, particularly the movement arts of Marceau, Barrault, Artauld, etc. I decided, for a bit of a giggle if you like, to book the hotel room where poor Wilde died which is in a now rather swish place called L'Hôtel. Having spent some time with his neglected masterpiece *Salomé*, which I love, I felt a strong affinity with Wilde and hoped I might make some contact with him. I fell into a fitful sleep and dreamed not of Wilde but of John Gielgud. During the dream I said, 'Sir John, I remember you in *The Ages of Man*', a brilliant one-man show based on Shakespeare's plays, and very moving it was. So in the dream Sir John says, 'Ah, you saw the show', and as if not sure whether to believe me, he asks me which was his first speech. Immediately I thought it must be 'Oh for a muse of fire' from the Chorus in *Henry V*, but of course it was not. I think in the dream he said it was Jacques's speech in *As You Like It* – the ages of man. So if I did not contact Wilde, I made contact with Gielgud, which is strange because I was not in any way obsessed by him in the same way I used to be about seeing Olivier.

I thought about this for some while and the following theory occurred to me. It is not possible to make contact with the other side unless you have met or known them. Since I have never met Oscar Wilde and could not know his voice, he would have to send an intermediary who would make the smallest bridge between us. And of course it would have to be Gielgud, who is our oldest living actor and whose connection with Wilde is very strong. He played successfully in *The Importance of Being Earnest* several times and he is related to Ellen Terry, the leading actress of Henry Irving, who was admired by Wilde. I thought this made a satisfactory interpretation, but then I discovered that Wilde had been obsessed with Gielgud's Aunt Ellen and had written poems to her! So in fact if Wilde wished to make contact with his acolyte, his twentieth-century interpreter of his most beautiful work, the only person he could possibly have sent would be Gielgud!

The première finishes with acclaim and when Amon makes a small speech to the audience and announces that the director is here, I walk on to the stage to the first bravos of the evening. I stand there at the end of the line, adopting a modest attitude, and am straightaway bolted into the middle by Mr Samsa. So I stand there and we do an uneven bow and then I flee to my dressing room where I pack away my few gifts. Susumi has given me a Canon camera that he saw me admiring when we went together to the Japanese inn in the mountains.

Before the run, I lay on the floor of my dressing room, just lying there and breathing in deeply and though I had no nerves I didn't want a repeat of this stomach cramp I had been getting when watching the show each night. So I lay there and felt at ease. I wandered into Masumi's room and he gave me a single red rose and then I went in to Mari and she gave me small porcelain cups in a beautiful wooden box, sake cups. Then Yoko gave me two wine-glass mats engraved with silver and then I went upstairs and watched the show.

After the show I expect something like the reception party given to Natalie Cole, where a whole banquet was laid out, but of course that was the opening celebration for the new theatre as well. So I anticipate a small party, perhaps, from Sphere, and flowing champagne. I imagine I'll see businessmen in black tie celebrating the arts as they did for Miss Cole, and even a small, delicate banquet. So in this expectation I don a jacket and enter the foyer, where I am at first shocked to see *plastic cups on the bar*! There are little cut-up corners of sandwiches, chocolate beans and sake in plastic cups. I am bitterly disappointed – it looks like the King's Head pub celebration for a lunch-time show. Speeches are then made and I trot out the usual clichés that erupt from my lips like bubbles from a fish. Of course, I mean it when I say I feel that the play has found its spiritual home here and after each fusillade of verbal mulch, Yoko translates, diving in and talking at great length like one of those piranha fish that eats everything in its path. I do admire her translating skill. Then Masumi very sweetly gives me an alarm-clock toy that beats a drum as the alarm goes off. This is to remind me of the family leaping into action when the clock starts beating. He gives me the toy publicly and so I have to squeeze the appropriate awkward grin between my bunched cheeks. Amon gives me a little Buddha, legs crossed and head bowed in perfect symmetry, made of wood. It could also be a Sumo wrestler in prayer before the event, muscles rippling in his crunched ball of energy. Then Masumi, true to his great skills as a part-time TV presenter, leads a cheer in a peculiar hand-clapping ceremony where we all start clapping with one finger, then two and then three until we are all clapping vigorously. It is fascinating since it seems as if the clapping has come from a distance and is now upon us. After the ceremonies are over we all repair to the café on the river and everybody is happy and it is warm enough to sit outside and take flashlight pictures and drink long gin and tonics with a blue haze around them, and we also eat sushi, a combination of different vegetables reconstructed into some gelatine mix. The cast are very happy and we sit by the still river which reflects a new moon. I know that now I have to be rid of this show for ever.

Thursday 12 November

This is the last time I eat my solitary breakfast at the Seiyo Hotel in the beautiful dining room where your every wish is attended to. The other half of the room is crowded with noisy Yankee businessmen; one is trumpeting through his nose like a walrus and of course I hear the buzz word 'scary'. It's over, and I leave via Bangkok to break my journey for one night and stay at the famous Oriental Hotel. I am becoming well known in Japan – this is my third show to be seen here in one year! And this is after writing last year in my autobiography that I envied all these British groups taking their Shakespeare to Tokyo. I have some of the best memories of Japan, plus some bad ones when I thought the minutes would never budge. I have enjoyed working the play into the new theatre, watching the production being shaped by lights and seeing it revealed once again, sensing it merge into a whole as the actors link, form tissues of communication together until they become one living organism, which is what a play should be. *Metamorphosis* becomes more and more a Japanese work as it sinks into their minds and their own culture. It becomes in places a ceremony, a dance, a ritual act played out each night.

Theatre can be a spiritual act in which all are enlightened by the experience and, if it is one motivated by the search for values, then the search is endless and full of surprises. There are many different ways to reach Nirvana. I like the craggy route and even if one deceives oneself at times in self-obsession, which is one of the hazards of this trade, one cannot deceive the audience. In the end I used Kafka to express me and the production to express Kafka. A marriage rather than a servant/master relationship . . . a marriage that produces an offspring that is a fine, red-blooded bastard and bears features of both parents, in fact the best of both. I have scattered Kafka's theatrical offspring round the world where they have always been welcome and thrived with the one exception – in New York, like so many poor creatures there, it was predictably mugged. In the end it is not so much a question of fidelity to a literal representation of Kafka as of another way of telling the story. But the story is essential and must in no way be diluted by being in a differently shaped bottle. I leave Japan speaking a smattering of Japanese and knowing that the latest offspring is well and happy in its new home!